The Peru Greys, a semi-pro baseball team, defeated the Chicago Cubs with a score of 3-2 in Peru in 1919. The game was arranged through the Cub's trainer, Peru native Andy Lotchaw. The Cubs later won the rematch with the Greys. The Greys were originally a C & O railroad team, then the Peru Community Association team and finally the Greys. The team, mostly composed of former professional baseball players, played on a farm where Peru High School now stands. As many as five thousand people would attend a game, paying fifty-five cents for a grandstand seat. Greys veteran Victor Aldridge went on to play for the Cubs, Pirates and Giants. Courtesy of the Miami County Historical Society.

*I*n 1886 we became THE local financial institution. In 1995 we still are. AmericanTrust Federal Savings Bank was established as the Peru Building and Loan in 1886. With 110 years of experience as the local, independent bank, we've made a commitment to North Central Indiana and are pleased to act as the corporate underwriter for *Miami County, Indiana.* With our corporate history and traditions so closely identified with Miami County, American Trust is proud to sponsor this publication that chronicles the past, illuminates the present, and offers a glimpse of the future. It is with a great sense of pride and gratitude that we dedicate this history of Miami County to the communities we serve, and to whom we owe our success.

AmericanTrust
FEDERAL SAVINGS BANK
20 WEST 5TH STREET   PERU, INDIANA 46970

Miami County, Indiana

A PICTORIAL HISTORY

BY MARILYN COPPERNOLL

THE DONNING COMPANY PUBLISHERS

Photo, previous spread: Peru hosted one of Indiana's first street fairs in 1894. This photograph of a small, steam-powered version of a roller coaster with Peru's second courthouse in the background was taken between 1894 and 1906 when the building was razed to make way for the present courthouse. The second courthouse was built in 1856. Courtesy of the Miami County Historical Society.

The Donning Company/Publishers
184 Business Park Drive, Suite 106
Virginia Beach, VA 23462

Steve Mull, General Manager
Bob Jonson, Project Director
Laura Hill, Project Research Coordinator
Mary Elizabeth Downing, Research Assistant
L. J. Wiley, Designer
Elizabeth Bobbitt, Executive Editor
Dawn V. Kofroth, Production Manager
Tony Lillis, Director of Marketing

Library of Congress Cataloging-in-Publication Data:
Coppernoll, Marilyn, 1956-
Miami County, Indiana: a pictorial history / by Marilyn Coppernoll.
    p. cm.
Includes bibliographical references and index.
ISBN 0-89865-951-5 (alk. paper)
1. Miami County (Ind.)—History—Pictorial works. 2. Miami County (Ind.)—History. I. Title
F532.M65C66 1995
              977.2'85—dc   95-33444
                                                        CIP

Printed in the United States of America

CONTENTS

PREFACE

We believe Miami County has many exciting and unusual stories from its past, and we hope as people read this book they will say of many things, "I didn't know that." This book is only the beginning, though. Miami County needs a comprehensive modern history. This book, because of the county's wealth of history, can only touch modern times in some places. This is a brief and colorful look at people and events that have shaped our county's development and its unique character. We have tried to include photographs and captions that entertain as well as inform. However, we received a wealth of old pictures for consideration which we certainly appreciated. Choosing among them was very difficult. Those who have recorded Miami County's history before us cannot be praised enough. Arthur Bodurtha and John Grahm, journalists and historians, left behind detailed accounts of people and events. Without their groundwork, researching this book would have been most difficult. The extensive knowledge of Miami County Museum archivist Joyce Miller and the material within museum archives certainly added to the book. A collection of interviews regarding county history with the people who recalled it or knew the facts provided numerous colorful facts and quotes.

We hope people with varying backgrounds and interests in history enjoy this book. There are probably errors. We want to know about our mistakes so succeeding descriptions of our past will be more accurate and we hope that readers will observe and record the times in which they live. We hope they will label their photographs and save their letters and diaries so that future historians will accurately tell their stories.

Facing page: This girl, circa 1912, was possibly wearing a sack dress made from a "Peerless" flour sack. The flour was sold by Charles E. Thorne and Son, Amboy. Courtesy of the Miami County Historical Society.

ACKNOWLEDGMENTS

Over eighty years have passed since Arthur Bodurtha wrote his history of Miami County. Members of the Miami County Historical Society and other people interested in preserving Miami County history have talked about publishing a more recent book. It just became a matter of the right people coming together at the right time to put this latest book together. However, without the support of American Trust Federal Savings Bank and that of the public, history might still be waiting on the book.

Putting together a pictorial history meant not only drawing upon the historical society's collection of photographs and illustrations, but those in private collections, and the public responded. People generously took the time to bring in their photographs for consideration and include as much information as possible. In doing so, they enriched the book in ways that would not have been possible without their contributions. We wish we had possessed the space to accept more for publication.

Six people comprised the committee that selected the photographs. Miami County Museum staff members Mildred Kopis, Joyce Miller, and Mary James met with historical society board members Jerry Wise and Ray Bakehorn and the author, Marilyn Coppernoll. A great deal of care and thought went into selecting the final photographs. Committee members also contributed many photographs, helped research information, and read the manuscript for historical accuracy.

Several people provided tidbits of information or observations in one form or another that made our book more accurate or more colorful. We hope this list is nearly complete: Charlet Smith, Paul Golden, Vesper Cook, Mildred Freeman, Bill Housouer, Velma Mongosa, Norma Richardson, Bill Richardson, Martin Roop, Herman Kinzie, Vera Zook, Noel Hunt, Lora Siders, Linda Schanlaub, Betty Stone, Bill Redmon, Bob Zimmerman, Steve Doud, Bill Oglesby, and Yvonne Hilgeman. Unless otherwise noted, quotes were drawn from the *Peru Tribune*.

Many, many people provided us with excellent photographs, making it difficult to choose the final ones for the book, and we regret not having room for more. Mary James did a wonderful job in reshooting original photographs, newspapers, and documents. In some cases her photographs made the originals look better. Thanks goes to Don Murphy for shooting the photographs of the author and the committee.

These women enjoyed swimming in the area of Bunker Hill. Courtesy of the Miami County Historical Society.

This mastodon skeleton was unearthed near Mexico and procured by C. F. Fites of Denver who sold it to the Milwaukee (Wisconsin) Museum. If the man had stood on the platform, his head would have just reached the lower jaw. Courtesy of the Miami County Historical Society.

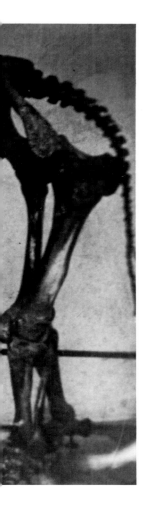

CHAPTER I

When Miami County Was Young

*T*housands of years ago the Kansan, Nebraskan, and Illinoian ice ages carved out Miami County's rolling hills and deep river valley, providing large sluiceways for glacial meltwaters. The great sluiceway that shaped the Mississinewa River also hewed out the natural wonder of the Liston Creek limestone formation called Seven Pillars, but the glaciers also left behind black muck and peat areas, sand and gravel deposits, and rich, fertile prairie land. Thus early man soon inhabited the area after the last glacier retreated.

Large Pleistocene animals like musk oxen and mastodons also lived in the area, for their bones have been found unearthed in Miami County. The animals may have been hunted by prehistoric man for the fluted points of Paleolithic man, dating back over ten thousand years, have also been discovered. Of significant prehistoric archeological interest is the All Seasons site discovered at Peru Industrial Park in 1984, which yielded a wealth of prehistoric information.

Ball State archeologists recovered pottery shards, points, stone tools, waste flakes, bone and burned bone, and deer antlers at the All Seasons site in Peru Industrial Park. Hearths, roasting pits, and undetermined soil stains were also recorded. The archeologists determined that the site, considered one of the most significant prehistoric archeological sites in northern Indiana, had been a multi-occupational one for over three thousand years. Courtesy of the Miami County Historical Society.

The abundance of game and fur-bearing animals plus the fertile soils of the prairies and river valley which attracted early man to the area also attracted the first Miami Indians for whom the county is named. They migrated from the area of Wisconsin and lived in the area over one hundred years before Indiana became a territory in 1800. Sixteen years later Indiana became a state, and about 1830, Miami Chief John B. Richardville sold land to pioneer Joseph Holman for five hundred dollars, "paid partly in trade instead of all cash." That land became the site of Miamisport.

Holman then sold 210 acres for five hundred dollars to William B. Hood, who established Peru shortly after Miami County was organized in 1834. A document describing the work of the surveyor and his assistants as they laid out Peru, states, ". . . the site was entirely covered with heavy timber and thick impenetrable growth of underbrush. Not a rod square was cleared. I have frequently heard Mr. Fisher say the men had to precede him and clear away the underbrush so he could get a sight through his instrument."

At the meeting of the commissioners who had been appointed to locate the county seat, Hood executed a bond. The bond provided for donation of a public square for a brick courthouse and log jail, on the condition that Peru became the county seat. History also hints that Hood offered Miamisport merchants lots in Peru if they relocated to Peru. By 1834 lots in Peru went up for sale. Taverns and hotels usually opened first followed by blacksmiths, carpenters, and dry goods stores. Trading posts sometimes maintained corrals where Indians could leave their ponies while they traded for goods.

Beyond Peru, settlers cut down timber to build cabins that often consisted of round, undressed logs with chunks in the cracks and mud daubed on. Clay, sticks, and packed mud earth made up chimneys. Then land was cleared for crops and livestock. However, food often meant eating fish, game, nuts, berries, and anything else the land provided, the same land that had supported the Miamis and other tribes in the area. But as more settlers moved in, a series of treaties forced the Miamis to give up more of their land.

An 1834 treaty dissolved the Eel River Reserve near Stockdale in northern Miami County on the Miami-Wabash County line. This forced some bands of Indians to move to other Indian reserves in the county. The federal government bought the land the Indians vacated so that the Wabash and Erie Canal could be completed through Miami County and other parts of Indiana. Yet even those acres weren't enough. More Indian reserves had to be given up in an 1838 treaty, and by 1840, a treaty not only forced the Miamis to cede more land, but called for their removal from Indiana by 1845. Some Miamis were excluded from removal, such as the family of Frances Slocum, a white woman who had married into the tribe, and the families of chiefs Richardville, Godfroy, and Meshingomesia. Other Miamis had intermarried with whites through the years.

The year 1845 came and went. Not enough Miamis had moved out of Indiana according to treaty requirements, so the federal government sent soldiers to remove the Miamis in 1846. Historical records vary in accounts as to how many Miamis were forced onto canal boats east of Peru, but a great many traveled until they reached a Kansas reservation. Eventually, though, white settlement of America's western frontier expanded until the Miamis were moved to an Oklahoma reservation which is represented in Miami, Oklahoma, today.

Indiana was growing and Miami County grew with it. Fourteen townships organized as more and more settlers arrived, clearing land of good timber which gave rise to numerous sawmills and decades later lured some factories to the county. The first log homes seldom exceeded sixteen by twenty feet and generally had only one room

Francis Godfroy, last Miami war chief, established a trading post east of Peru in 1823. Though he died in 1840, his family members were permitted by the federal government to remain in Indiana while many other Miamis were removed to a Kansas reservation. Godfroy's home still stands east of Peru today near the Godfroy Cemetery which was placed on the National Register of Historic Places in 1984. Courtesy of the Miami County Historical Society.

Miami Indian Chief John B. Richardville received several sections of land from the federal government in an 1826 treaty. He later sold to Joseph Holman for five hundred dollars one section on which Miamisport was established with one street named Richardville. Richardville's family was excluded from removal in 1846 to a Kansas reservation. Courtesy of an anonymous donor.

Seven Pillars stands east of Peru on the north side of the Mississinewa River. The Miami Indians established an early trading post there where they hosted meetings and dances. Later the Pillars served as a favorite picnic spot for church and other groups until about the 1950s. Note the man standing in front and a buggy off to the right. Courtesy of the Miami County Historical Society.

with a sleeping loft. Sometimes when several families arrived together, they lived in one cabin until others could be built. Because money was scarce on the frontier and hired labor was seldom depended on, the settlers would swap "work" with each other. By doing that, neighbors for miles around helped each other raise cabins and barns.

Many of the settlers came by covered wagon drawn by oxen or on horseback from as far away as Virginia, New York, Ohio, and Pennsylvania. Later, as the Wabash and Erie Canal extended farther and farther westward, immigrants arrived in Miami County. They either arrived in the county's early years to help build the canal or traveled on it to find new homes and set up new businesses. And with the arrival of canal boats came not only more settlers, but furniture and other goods that brought a kind of civilization from the East to a young county not far removed from what became the wild frontier of the West.

The National Hotel, reportedly Peru's first hotel, stood on the northeast corner of Canal and Miami Streets. Built around 1835, it had forty rooms. Passengers from the first canal boat, the Indiana, *which had to stop a mile above Peru, stayed at the hotel. Hotels of the period offered beds filled with "prairie grass" and meals that included "deer, turkeys, pheasants, squirrels, and fish." A substantial meal usually cost a quarter while lodging for a week might cost a dollar. Courtesy of the Miami County Historical Society.*

This 1866 map of Miami County shows the layout of Peru and other communities in existence at the time. Some of the communities like Xenia, now called Converse, were noted with their original names. Courtesy of the Miami County Historical Society.

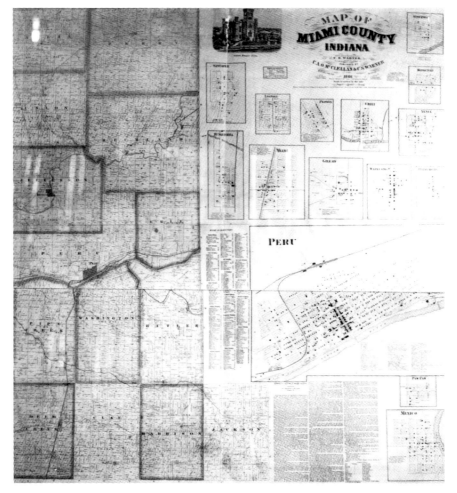

German-born Moses Falk, one of the community's first settlers, established this log trading post near Butler Township's Peoria in 1837. Falk traded with the Indians for some years before moving to Peru in 1850 and establishing a business. His son, Julius, reportedly became one of the most widely known clothiers in northern Indiana. Courtesy of the Miami County Historical Society.

The Peru Chamber of Commerce erected a stone marker at the Stranger's Grave in 1908. The grave is the final resting place of Eli Macy who, as a stranger to Miami County in 1830, drowned while crossing the swollen Wabash River near Godfroy's trading post. The marker replaced an earlier one near the spot where Macy's body washed up at what is now the riverbank between the old C&O Railroad shops and West City Park. Years ago local folklore suggested that if one put an ear to the grave and asked Macy what he wanted, he would say, "Nothing." And nothing was all he ever said. Courtesy of the Miami County Historical Society.

This Cary log cabin, built in the 1840s, was typical of many early county homes. Cary, located in Harrison Township, faded away in importance after 1867 when the Pan Handle Railroad was completed and helped the nearby town of Amboy grow. Courtesy of the Miami County Historical Society.

The Long family homestead, built in Peoria, once served as a tavern. Courtesy of the Miami County Historical Society.

The Lafayette Flagg home was the first house built in Washington Township which was established in 1843 and named for George Washington. Flagg taught at the nearby Flagg School sometime after 1876. Courtesy of the Miami County Historical Society.

Top photo: These men established lives in Miami County's early days, then journeyed to California where they made their fortunes as '49ers. The term refers to those people who were involved in some way with the 1849 California gold rush. Seated left to right are: J. T. Stevens, J. T. Henton, J. O. Cole, George Rettig, and Judge John Mitchell. Courtesy of the Miami County Historical Society.

John Fitzgibbon painted the original canvas of this limited edition print showing the removal of Miami Indians onto canal boats. The families of Chiefs Richardville, Godfroy, Meshingomesia, Lafontaine, and white woman Frances Slocum, who had married a Miami chief, were excluded by treaty from removal to a Kansas reservation 1845 and later to Oklahoma. When many Miamis stayed on in Indiana, the federal government sent soldiers to remove them in 1846. An oral account of the removal east of Peru has been passed down through the generations. "It was a sad day. They were hugging each other and crying, and picking up dirt to take with them," reported Lora Siders, historian for the Miami Nation of Indians of Indiana. Print courtesy of Floyd E. Leonard, Chief of the Miami Tribe of Oklahoma.

This is how part of Broadway appeared in Peru, circa 1860s, much like any Old West town. Courtesy of the Louanna Wilson Estate.

This photograph shows George Helderle's saloon, reportedly Peru's first, located on the west side of Broadway between Second and Canal Streets in about 1866. Helderle is named and may be the one wearing a white apron. Note the barely visible Peru Brewery sign hanging to the left of the batwing doors. "Among the many saloonists catering to the daily luxuries of our public, none are more ably administering to the pleasures and wants of our friends than George F. Helderle from whom we obtain our finest foreign and domestic wines, liquors and fragrant cigars . . ." from A Description of the City of Peru, *published in 1897. Courtesy of the Miami County Historical Society.*

This is how the east side of Broadway, looking north, appeared in Peru in the 1860s. The courthouse in the background, which stood where the courthouse does now at Broadway and Main, resembled an English, Norman-style keep. Courtesy of the Miami County Historical Society.

Mr. and Mrs. Lawrence (Bruiser) Fewell and their child stand in front of their blacksmith shop in Clay Township's Loree after 1888 when the village became a stop on the Pan Handle Railroad. Blacksmith shops were among the earliest businesses to spring up in the county. Loree, which also had a sawmill and general store, eventually faded away. Courtesy of Jackie J. Pearcy.

This flood photograph was taken from the south side of the Wabash River looking northwest toward Peru in the 1870s. Note the houses in the water. Bodurtha's 1914 history states that the first major flood after the county was settled occurred in 1847, then again in 1883, and twice in 1904. "But the floods . . . all sink into insignificance when brought into comparison with the great flood of March, 1913." Courtesy of the Miami County Historical Society.

J. L. Hetzner owned and operated the Peru Bicycle Arcade in the Zern building on West Main Street in the 1890s. Riding bicycles was not only a pastime, but a form of transportation. Courtesy of the Miami County Historical Society.

CHAPTER 2

Transportation and Communication

*T*rail blazes cut into trees served as early "road signs," but not until the county commissioners first met in 1834 was there a petition for construction of a road. Residents asked for a road between Peru and Mexico. Early surveys for state roads led to some roads opening and being improved. Early settlers, however, "cut out" most of the roads along the proposed routes, and it became the county's responsibility to improve them. The first such road cut out in Miami County was Strawtown Pike which ran from Strawtown in Hamilton County to Miamisport. Other roads were constructed leading from Peru to Chili, Paw Paw, and Xenia, later named Converse.

This Great Western auto in front of the Bearss Hotel at Third and Broadway was built in a factory located in the Oakdale addition which Peru annexed for commercial development about 1906. Great Western, originally named Model Automobile Company, acquired its new name about 1908 and employed forty-three people who could produce three hundred cars a year. However, Great Western declared bankruptcy in 1916. Courtesy of Jerry Wise.

However, in Miami County's youth, waterways provided the main arteries of transportation, chief among them the Wabash and Erie Canal. Construction started on the canal in New York about 1832 and progressed steadily westward with canal workers often earning "sixty cents a day plus whiskey." Generally these workers included people of German and Irish nationalities. However, the canal not only brought emigrant labor but emigrant and native-born families looking to build new homes and open new businesses. An alternate canal route following the Eel River in northern Miami County had been surveyed, but the Wabash River route won, possibly because businessmen already established at Peru pressed for it. Such men knew the canal trade would increase their business and thus their profits. Certainly the opening of the canal as far as Peru along the Wabash contributed to the county's growth.

The first canal boat was to arrive in Peru on July 4, 1837, but the county's first newspaper, the *Peru Forester*, reported, "Before 12 o'clock that day, the town was filled with people of the county to witness the grand display to be made on that occasion. Unfortunately, the boats did not arrive. The canal banks, being porous, absorbed the water much faster than was anticipated." Two years before, the *Science*, the first steamboat to arrive in Peru on the Wabash, had come and gone without fanfare.

Just as transportation in the county expanded the early settlers' horizons in travel, early newspapers expanded their horizons of knowledge. Some months after the *Peru Forester* folded in 1839, the *Peru Gazette* began dispensing news and then split into a second newspaper, the *Peru-Democrat*. Both newspapers survived until 1842 when the humorous *Cork Screw* was published anonymously by "Nehemiah, Hezekiah, and Obadiah." It folded, however, in less than a year. The *Peru Republican* began publishing in 1856. The first daily newspaper, the *Daily Miami County Sentinel*, folded after a month in 1854. It would be 1884 before a newspaper, the *Peru Evening Journal*, became a successful afternoon daily.

A ferry carried passengers and freight across the Wabash River at Peru until the first bridge was built in 1843. This photograph shows South Broadway as it met the bridge over the Wabash and Erie Canal. In turn, the new bridge linked with the covered bridge over the Wabash. Eventually the canal fell into disuse, and the covered bridge was dismantled in 1879. Miami County eventually had a total of six covered bridges. Courtesy of the Louanna Wilson Estate.

The Andrew Petty family pose by their home in Pettysville in the 1890s. Daniel Petty platted the village along the Eel River in Richland Township in 1872 when the Vandalia Railroad was built. From left to right are: Eugenia, Tisa, Alva, and Andrew. Sam Adamson, who sold dry goods, groceries, and other items, sits on the huckster wagon with which he transported his wares to customers. Pettysville had a general store and grain elevator, but it eventually died away. Courtesy of Dorothy and Weldon Klepinger

Meanwhile, the public sale of former Indian lands, beginning in 1840, encouraged more people to move in and homestead. The Wabash and Erie Canal, however, had become too expensive to maintain, and earlier sections of it had fallen into disrepair. Though plans to complete the canal were carried out, the first "Iron Horses" already smoked and chugged along rails across Indiana before the canal era waned to a close in the 1870s. Railroads opened the state to even more settlement, and Miami County was no exception. Roads continued to expand and improve in the county; some of which contributed to the commercial growth of Allen Township's Five Corners, so named for its intersection of roads leading in five different directions. However, one of the first railroads to reach Peru, the Lake Erie and Western Railroad in 1854, opened up new business opportunities for the county seat. Mexico experienced a revival when the Eel River Railroad, later called the Vandalia, laid tracks across northern Miami County in the 1870s.

Other communities benefited from the railroads, too. The villages of Bennetts Switch, Birmingham, Wagoner, and Courter began as stations on the Lake Erie and Western Railroad. Jefferson Township's

This collage shows some of Miami County's early newspapers. Courtesy of the Miami County Historical Society.

Doyle developed as a siding on the railroad for farmers shipping livestock. However, those villages, except for Bennetts Switch, eventually faded away. The Lake Erie and Western contributed to the demise of Wooleytown by helping Denver and diverted trade from Perrysburg which had served as a trade center. The Eel River Railroad, completed through the county in 1872, contributed not only to the revival of Mexico, but to the birth of Denver and Pettysville. However, the railroad also took trade away from the village of Paw Paw, which eventually died off, and contributed to the decline of commerce in Gilead and Chili.

Chili's business also declined because of the Peru and Detroit Railroad in 1886. The Indianapolis, Peru and Chicago Railroad took trade from Gilead, too, but kept Macy going. Deedsville, which began as a warehouse on a farm on line with the new road, profited from the Cincinnati, Chicago and Louisville Railroad, more popularly called the "Huckleberry Line." However, because the railroad bypassed it, Union City, located two miles west of Deedsville, perished. The Peru and Indianapolis Railroad helped create Leonda one mile north of Bunker Hill, but the Pan Handle Railroad, crossing the Lake Erie and Western at Bunker Hill, later took Leonda's business away.

The Pan Handle Railroad, completed about 1867, led to Amboy, McGrawsville, and Loree becoming rail stations. Loree died off as did Urbana and Snow Hill, which were located in Harrison Township. The railroad brought growth and prosperity to Bunker Hill and a boom period for Converse, too, but led to the decline of Santa Fe. Completion of the Chesapeake and Ohio Railroad, however, led to construction of a rail station called New Santa Fe, located about a mile north of the old town, and many businesses subsequently moved there.

John A. Graham, who wrote **Pioneer History of Peru and Miami County** *in 1877, was elected county sheriff and appointed clerk in the Wabash and Erie Canal land office in 1846. He later issued the first edition of the* **Miami County Sentinel.** *He served as delegate to the state convention to form a new state constitution, and was special U.S. agent to pay annuities to the Miamis in 1857 and 1859. Courtesy of the Miami County Historical Society.*

The railroad hospital opened in 1885 on what was called "Flax Hill," now North Broadway. The Sisters of Charity provided the nursing. The dining room and kitchen were known for having "both hot and cold water." The hospital was torn down to make room for the present Peru High School which opened in 1971. Courtesy of the Miami County Historical Society.

Peru's Wayne Street Bridge over the Wabash River is shown here under construction about 1905. When completed, it was reportedly the longest concrete bridge in the world at that time—about seven hundred feet. Courtesy of the Miami County Historical Society.

Peru saw its first telephone exchange in 1881, eight years before residents organized the Peru and Detroit Railroad, and leased it to the Wabash Railroad, which ran between Peru and Chili. The railroad then built a roundhouse, shops, and a hospital for railroad employees. However, the abandoned Peru and Detroit tracks and right-of-way paved the way for the Winona Traction Line to offer interurban service. Its interurban cars connected Miami County in 1906 with the Chicago, South Bend and Northern Indiana Electric Railway at Goshen in Elkhart County.

The Wabash River Traction Company, later called the Fort Wayne and Northern Traction Company, connected Miami County with Lafayette to the west and Fort Wayne to the east about 1903. In 1902 the Indianapolis Northern Traction Company received a right-of-way through southern Miami County.

Following in the wake of interurban cars came electric cars. The idea of steam cars drew attention in the early 1920s, but only briefly, because interest in gasoline-powered cars had already grown. Yet horses drawing wagons and buggies could still be found trotting alongside interurban cars, bicycles, and "horseless carriages."

Many trains still chugged through the county in the 1920s, transporting goods and passengers. In the Depression years of the 1930s, trains carried hobos as well as freight. Hobos often traveled from one town to the next, looking for any little job that might provide them with food for a little while at least. When there was no work, they begged for food or scrounged for scraps of meat and vegetables.

Peru resident Bob Zimmerman remembered living a "life on the rails during the Depression," traveling from Indiana to Texas, Arizona, Louisiana, and back again. "We were hoboing not because we liked it, but because we wanted a job," he said, recollecting his hobo years.

Brown Commercial Car Company, which located in Peru's Oakdale addition in 1912, also manufactured Brown funeral cars. Courtesy of Jerry Wise.

This train wrecked over the Wabash River near Peru. Courtesy of the Miami County Historical Society.

J. E. Muhfield designed the Mallet engine while general superintendent of motive power for the Baltimore and Ohio Railroad. "Old Maud," possibly nicknamed after a strong-pulling comic strip mule of the time, was the "longest and most powerful steam locomotive in the world" when it first rolled down a track in 1904. The engine revolutionized steam transportation because it increased the tonnage freight trains could haul. Courtesy of the Miami County Historical Society.

This crew from Miami was work-ing on an Indiana Union Traction line which connected Peru with the neighboring county seat of Kokomo in 1902. A year earlier the Indianapolis Northern Trac-tion Company received the right-of-way through southern Miami County. In 1904 the Winona Interurban Railway also served Peru. The last interurban left Peru around 1938. Courtesy of Jackie J. Pearcy.

This was the Miami railroad depot looking south from Fulton Street. Note the signs advertising Western Union Telegraph and Cable Office and Sunday School excursions. Courtesy of Jackie J. Pearcy.

Arthur L. Bodurtha, who wrote the 1914 History of Miami County, Indiana, *sits in his office at the* Peru Journal. *He bought a half interest in the newspaper in 1891 and sold it in 1913. He was admitted to the bar of the Miami Circuit Court in 1889, but abandoned law for journalism two years later and became well known throughout Indiana as an editorial writer. Courtesy of the Miami County Historical Society.*

Men change a streetlight near Broadway and Canal in 1910. Note the interurban car on the left. The building in the center, which served as a rail depot and stop for the Indiana Traction Company, has been restored. It now provides space for a number of community social events. The Commercial Hotel and restaurant, shown on the right, stood where the Literary Aid Society building stands now on West Canal. Courtesy of Jerry Wise.

Edith Moseley, left, and Hattie Stutesman stand beside the first electric car in Peru in 1912. Courtesy of the Louanna Wilson Estate.

Interurban cars and a horse-drawn wagon battle their way through snow on Broadway in Peru. Courtesy of the Miami County Historical Society.

This is the last remaining of six steam cars built in 1918 by Bryan Steam Corporation which relocated from New Mexico to Peru and still exists today. This car was produced for the sales manager. Arthur Wissinger of Denver bought the car in 1927 and "drove it for years as a family car, winter and summer." He eventually sold it to someone out of state. Growing interest in gasoline engines put an end to the production of steam cars. *Courtesy of the Miami County Historical Society.*

This was the interior of Miller Tires complete with price lists for tires sold at the time. *Courtesy of the Miami County Historical Society.*

These people pose with an airplane at Peru Airport, possibly in the 1920s or later. The word "Peru" appears on the roof of the building in the background. Peru has a municipal airport today. *Courtesy of the Miami County Historical Society.*

Peru's WARU radio tower went up in 1954 and the station went on the air. From left to right are Wendell Hansen, V. J. Finster, Harold Speicker, Jack Brookbank, A. C. Bernstein, Susannah Rush, William T. Wallace, Don Cooper, Willard Redmon, and Joseph Marburger. *Courtesy of the Miami County Historical Society.*

This photograph was taken just minutes after the First National Bank at Main and Broadway in Peru was robbed on October 18, 1929. The Peru Republican reported "seven, fashionably dressed bandits stole $57,575.67 in cash and $17,245.15 worth of negotiable securities . . . at about 11:30 o'clock that morning." The bank, reputedly Miami County's oldest, was established in 1864. Courtesy of the Miami County Historical Society.

CHAPTER 3

Communities

"Someone of the surveying party asked Hood what he was going to call his town and he replied that he didn't care, so long as it was a short name. A number of names were suggested and they finally agreed on Peru." This explanation of Peru's name might or might not be true, but the town grew and eventually swallowed up Miamisport whose founder had once sported dreams of making it the county seat. Peru incorporated in February 1848, sponsored its first election in March, and levied a tax of fifteen cents on each one hundred dollars of property in April for town purposes. Peru also began setting town ordinances, one of which early on regarded hogs running loose on the streets. "For nearly two years the legal learning, the broad statesmanship and the burning eloquence of our city fathers boiled and seethed around the question of hogs, to impound them or let them run. Ordinance after ordinance was framed, but there always seemed a crack through which a pig could crawl," said John Graham, county historian and mayor of Peru.

These children wait in the back of a horse-drawn wagon on Peru's dirt Broadway around 1900. Broadway was paved about 1902. Courtesy of the Miami County Historical Society.

Town records of April 26, 1850, state that Oliver Dyer, marshal, reported the sale of fifty-two hogs impounded by him. The record then continued with, "Comes now the said Oliver Dyer and presents a claim to the mayor and council for impounding, advertising and feeding fifty-two hogs, amounting to $29.25, with a credit thereon of $1.80, being the amount realized from the sale of said hogs."

As the bill was presented, a man presented a petition "numerously signed by citizens of the corporation, praying for the repeal of the hog law." The mayor and council repealed the "hog law." A similar ordinance was introduced later, though, while cows had run of Peru's streets until around 1892 when the council, after much discussion that sometimes grew heated, passed an ordinance prohibiting livestock of any kind from running loose within corporate limits.

Though a proposal to establish a municipal water works first came before the town board in 1871, the board didn't act upon it until 1878. Meanwhile, H. E. and C. F. Sterne and Company started construction of a gas plant in connection with their woolen mills. Later the Peru-American Gas Company incorporated, bought the plant in 1886, and improved it. A year earlier, electric lights had lit up Peru for the first time. However, it wasn't until after 1900 that the electric plant became one of few municipally owned ones. The *Peru Tribune*, still published today, began publishing in 1921.

The village of Ridgeview, described by the *Peru Republican* in 1898 as possessing "one dozen houses, a railway hospital and a mail box" with a "ridge view" of Peru, adjoined Peru's north corporate limits. It was sometimes referred to as the "Bearss settlement" because Daniel Bearss settled there over fifty years before and several family members still resided there in the 1890s. Peru annexed the settlement as well as the village of South Peru in 1914.

South Peru, which stands on the south side of the Wabash River, was platted independently of the county seat in 1873 by Elizabeth, Maria, Rachel, and Laban Armstrong, and William Erwin, Elizabeth's husband. Two years earlier Maris Wheel Factory had located there, but was later converted to a furniture factory. Other industries included a brewery, a packing house, and Cliffton brickyards which produced much of the early brick that paved Peru.

Mexico, laid out by John B. and Simeon Wilkinson, is the county's second oldest community. Early businesses included a trading post, blacksmiths, a tannery, a tailor, and a cabinet maker. The River House served as Mexico's first hotel, and the *Mexico Herald* was published.

Peru's 1913 flood left debris behind on Peru's Warren Street. The high water mark on the trees was fifteen feet high. "Peru is flooded from one end to the other. They are using boats on Broadway . . . Yesterday they got a boat from Wabash and an Indian came along. He rescued all the people that were saved : . . People were upstairs waving handkerchiefs and shooting guns, trying to attract people's attention . . . They screamed for help, but everyone was afraid to venture out in the river. Houses of all kinds floated down river . . . ," wrote Esther Saine in a letter to her brother, Dick Saine, March 26, 1913. Courtesy of the Miami County Historical Society.

Edmund O'Brian, born in Ireland in 1852, is shown on Peru's courthouse square in this photograph taken about two years before his death in 1941. In 1915 O'Brian became the first person cited under the new ordinance against jaywalking. Courtesy of the Miami County Historical Society.

The *Orphan* was published by the Mexico Orphans' home in the 1890s. Mexico once also boasted a public school, a large woolen mill, a bank, and several general, hardware, and implement stores.

John R. Wilkinson and Matthew Fenimore laid out Perrysburg in 1837. Within two years the village claimed a trading post, a tavern, a store, a physician, and a blacksmith. Later a hotel and public school opened, as did a brick and tile factory.

Chili, originally named New Market, was laid out by Jesse Mendenhall in 1839. Soon a store with a post office, a harness shop, and a doctor located there. In later years a roller mill, grain elevator, and school opened. The *Chili Weekly* published in 1895. An old settlers' association, established sometime in the late 1800s, still held its annual picnic for members of pioneer families at Chili as late as 1914. Around 1900 Chili maintained a telephone exchange, a telegraph office, and an express office.

Gilead, founded around 1840, owes its existence to founder Adam E. Rhodes. A doctor immediately located an office there followed by a blacksmith shop, a steam sawmill, a tanyard, and a hotel. The completion of the Indianapolis, Peru and Chicago Railroad and the Eel River Railroad led to a decline in some of Gilead's business though it still maintained its post office.

After 1900, business revived when the Winona Interurban Railway was completed. Around 1910 Gilead boasted a sawmill, two general stores, and a public school.

Once described as a "wide spot in the road" with its biggest event being the annual spring and fall tenderloin suppers, Erie has no marked town limits. It had a post office and the community war-

ranted construction of the Erie Consolidated School in 1917, now used as a community building where the tenderloin suppers are held.

Santa Fe is the reason Santa Claus, Indiana, has its name. Ebenezer Fenimore laid out Santa Fe in 1845, but the other town was laid out about 1890 and wanted to take the name of Santa Fe. However, the U.S. Post Office stipulated no two towns in the same state could have the same name. So the later town took the name of Santa Claus. As for Santa Fe, it boasted a general store, a sawmill, a school, and perhaps half a dozen houses within two years of its establishment.

Isaac Litzenberger, who opened the first store in Peoria, established the village along the Mississinewa River in 1845. A short while

The William Philabaum home at Erie, shown in this 1978 photograph, had a store and Erie's post office in its front room. A trading post to trade with the Indians was established in 1827, but the township wasn't organized until 1839. Though the township may have been named for an early settler, "Black Hawk" Henton, the township's name changed to Erie in 1847. Courtesy of the Miami County Historical Society.

This is Chili's elevator in Richland Township, which was established in 1837 and named for the "fertility of its soil." Courtesy of the Miami County Historical Society.

later a doctor located there. Peoria served as a trade center of some importance until the railroads came through the county.

Waupecong, sometimes spelled "Wawpecong," originally had the name of White Hall when laid out by James Highland, Jacob Hight and Andrew Petty in 1849. Other people came to set up a doctor's office, stores, a sawmill, and a steam flour mill.

Converse, laid out by O. H. P. Macy and Willis Elliott in 1849, was originally called Xenia. Henry Overman built the first house, a log structure, on the Delphi Road which later became Miami Street. A general store and hotel opened, and a carpenter and cabinetmaker set up businesses. Eventually an opera house opened, too. Additions were platted onto Xenia through 1867 when the town experienced a boom thanks to completion of the Pan Handle Railroad. Sawmills, a stave factory, and a planing mill and a flax mill opened. The *Xenia Gazette*, was published in 1868, followed by the *Xenia Times* in 1879, and the *Converse Clipper* and *Xenia Journal* in 1883. The last eventually became the *Converse Journal*, and was published as late as 1914.

In 1873 plats were surveyed for tax purposes and filed under the name of Converse. The fire department organized in 1885. The discovery of natural gas in the late 1880s brought in a brief business boom.

Alexander Blake built the first house and sawmill in Miami shortly after it was laid out in 1849. In 1879, a number of the county's original settlers from southern Miami, and from Cass and Howard Counties formed the Tri-County Old Settlers' Association, which still met in Miami as of 1914. In the early 1900s, Miami supported a tile factory, two general stores, and a grain elevator among its businesses.

Bunker Hill was platted by James Myers, John Duckwall, and Alexander Galbraith in 1851. Myers built the first house. A post office opened along with a store at Fourth and Main Streets. Dr. Hubbard, who served as the town's first doctor, reportedly "carried his medicines in a small tin pail" and was "never in too big a hurry" to trade horses on his way to visit a patient. Another doctor, James A. Meek, may be said to have "stolen" a post office for Bunker Hill. The town had no post office when Meek arrived, but the village of Leonda, located one mile north, did. Bunker Hill residents reportedly got tired of having to go to Leonda for their mail, tobacco, and other sundries. Thus Meek rode horseback to Leonda one night, confiscated the post office supplies and equipment, and brought them back in his saddlebags. The railroads were informed to pick up the mail at Bunker Hill thereafter while Meek became the town's first post master in 1858. Leonda gradually died away.

About 1865 a tin shop opened and a cabinetmaker set up shop. The first hotel opened in 1868 near the junction of the Lake Erie and Pan Handle Railroads, and a sawmill opened. The first hardware store opened a year after the *Village News* began publication around 1871.

Gilead's Madeford Hotel, built in 1835, became the home of Mrs. Ella Siegfred in Perry Township. Perry Township, established in 1837, was named for Commodore Oliver H. Perry. Courtesy of the Miami County Historical Society.

This was a mill at Peoria in Butler Township, possibly from the 1930s. Peoria also had a post office called "Reserve" because of an Indian reserve which lay just above the village. Butler Township, established about 1841, had several Miami Indian reserves. Courtesy of the Miami County Historical Society.

In 1874 the newspaper became the *Bunker Hill News*, then the *Independent Press*, and finally in 1880 the *Bunker Hill Press*. For a short time beginning in 1893, the agricultural paper *Stock and Farm* was published in connection with the *Press* until the latter moved to Peru and became the *Miami County Record*. After the *Press* moved, Bunker Hill published the *Sword* for about three months and issued the new *Bunker Hill Press* beginning in 1895. The *Farm Spokesman* was published as late as 1941.

North Grove, when platted out by William North in 1854, was originally called Moorefield. The community became known as North Grove about the time additions were platted to it in 1867. A store and a blacksmith shop opened not long after the town was laid out. North Grove had two grain elevators, a general store, a public school, and a post office.

George and Anderson Wilkinson laid out Macy, originally called Lincoln, in 1860. A blacksmith shop, a store, a hotel, and a steam sawmill opened shortly thereafter. Two doctors also opened offices. By 1869 the town had grown so rapidly additions were made to it. The first drug and clothing stores soon located there, and the Five

Corners post office moved to Lincoln. However, there already existed a post office called Lincoln in adjoining Cass County. Thus in 1875, residents petitioned the Miami County Commissioners to change the town name to Macy after president of the Indianapolis, Peru and Chicago Railroad, David Macy.

Macy's newspaper, the *Monitor*, was first published in 1885 and continued through 1914. For a time the town maintained a local telephone company, several general stores, hardware and implement stores, a hotel, an elevator, and telegraph and express offices.

John Ptomey, Bennett (or Barnett) Fellows, John A. Lamb, and Abijah Ridgeway laid out Amboy in 1867. Two sawmills were built followed by a store and a gristmill, and several doctors located there. The Amboy Academy, built in 1872, offered Latin, Greek, rhetoric, civics, and geology among other subjects. The *Amboy-Independent* began publication in 1902 and continued through 1914. Amboy once maintained Home Telephone Company, a large canning factory, a creamery, a flour mill, a lumber yard, and various stores.

This undated photograph shows a Bunker Hill grocery store in Pipe Creek Township. Courtesy of the Miami County Historical Society.

This tintype, circa 1860s, shows Jesse Gettinger Sr. at left and Isaac Herrell seated outside an old store building in Miami in Deer Creek Township. Herrell laid out the town on land he bought from the government. Gettinger settled on land adjoining Herrell's. The township, established in 1847, lay in the heart of the Miami Indians' "Big Reserve." Courtesy of Jackie J. Pearcy.

This was a North Grove drugstore, circa 1910. The town, standing in Harrison Township, was incorporated in 1912, then unincorporated in 1987. The township, named for President William Harrison, was formed in 1846. Courtesy of the Miami County Historical Society.

William Deeds built a warehouse on his farm on the line of the new railroad in 1869 to handle grain and produce. Someone else built a store near the warehouse, but Deedsville wasn't actually laid out until 1870 by Albert Deeds and Samuel M. Leedy. The town once maintained a creamery, a public school house, and a post office.

Bennetts Switch, established as a station on the Lake Erie and Western Railroad in the late 1860s, stood on land belonging to Baldwin M. Bennett. Around 1914, the Indiana Union Traction Company extended its line through the community. At that time Bennett's Switch supported two general stores, a grain elevator, and some other businesses.

Denver, laid out by Harrison Grimes in 1872, originally extended from Jefferson Township into Union and Richland Townships, but a petition to the county commissioners asked them to change township lines so Denver would stand entirely in Jefferson Township. The man who built the first Denver residence also opened the first business—a blacksmith shop. Next came a store and a sawmill followed by planing and flour mills. By 1876 Denver College opened and in 1883, the first issue of the *Denver Sun* newspaper appeared. The *Denver Tribune* was established in 1897 and published through 1914. At that time Denver shipped large quantities of grain and other farm products, and supported a large basket factory, stores, a public school, and a post office.

McGrawsville began as a station on the Pan Handle Railroad in the 1870s, but Nelson McGraw built a small store there two years before that. The community's principal attractions after 1900 included a post office, store, and sawmill.

Though many villages, sometimes consisting of only a few houses

and maybe a business or two, developed early then faded away, Tincup is an exception. In 1962 Fay Longstreth had trouble directing people to his place of business four miles north of Peru on State Road 19. So, after visiting his sister in Tincup, Colorado, he decided to call the little cluster of houses and his business on the curves Tincup.

This is an early downtown scene of Bennetts Switch. Courtesy of Ned Reyburn.

Lewis Coustin, seated on his hearse, and his brother pose outside their Denver funeral home in 1898. Courtesy of the Miami County Historical Society.

This was how Allen Township's Macy looked before 1914. Allen Township was established in 1859. Courtesy of Forest (Bud) Zartman.

Top photo: This aerial view of Clay Township's McGrawsville was taken in 1946. The town became a station on the Pan Handle Railroad after it was completed about 1867. The arrow points out the church. Courtesy of Rhonda Blackburn.

CHAPTER 4

Churches

Early on, as Miami County residents built homes and founded communities, but sometimes before that, their interest turned to forming religious groups and constructing places of worship. That widespread early interest is reflected in the wealth of churches found today.

Robert Miller and Edward J. Kidd and their families arrived in 1837 in the area where Paw Paw village would be established in eastern Richland Township. After settling their families in, Kidd and Miller, with axes over their shoulders, set out for Peru to find a minister. "They blazed a trail left by Indians," according to one account, "and followed that trace to Peru. The pastor of the Peru circuit, which included all of the territory from below Logansport to Fort Wayne, was given directions, that he might call on the new community." Within a few days, the minister was spotted riding down the trail toward the Miller and Kidd homes. The Methodist church organized and met in a school until an actual church was built in 1846. The story of how the Kidd and Miller families found a pastor ech-

Harry G. Fetter, who took this photograph, decorated the altar of the Presbyterian Church on President Lincoln's death on April 15, 1865. Courtesy of the Miami County Historical Society.

oes similar experiences that other early pioneers lived when Miami County was young. In some cases, church societies organized long before their communities did. The village of Paw Paw, for example, was not platted and recorded until 1847.

Long before the first families settled in Miami County, Jesuit priests traveled amongst the Indians of the Wabash Valley, trying to convert them to Christianity. French traders, who were often Catholic, sometimes acted as missionaries in the valley and said masses at trading posts for the earliest settlers. Thus it's not surprising that Catholics organized the first church group in Miami County.

When Peru was laid out, two lots on the northwest corner of Fifth and Miami Streets were donated for a Catholic church. In 1860 ground for the Catholic Cemetery was bought and consecrated. In 1865 Catholic priests offered services in Bunker Hill, and a church organized in 1870. However, though a frame house of worship was built, the congregation disbanded.

The Paw Paw Methodist Church was named for the village of Paw Paw. The first Methodists met at a private home, then organized a society and built a church. The church, listed on the National Historic Register, is one of the longest continually operating churches in northern Indiana. Paw Paw Pike bridge leading to the church from the south, is one of the few remaining iron bridges left in Indiana. Courtesy of the Miami County Historical Society.

Unlike Catholic Church groups, Methodist congregations seemed to form throughout the county. William M. Reyburn, who homesteaded a farm where West City Park is now, settled in Peru in 1831 and conducted Methodist services in the homes of local residents until a house of worship was finished in 1836. Near Mexico, Methodist services were held in a home beginning in 1833 until a frame house for worship was built. The Chili Methodist Church, organized about 1839, offered services in members' homes until about 1845. The Macy Methodist Church organized eighteen years before Macy was established in 1860. A year earlier, the Methodist Church organized at Gilead, though services had been performed in members' homes beginning seven or eight years before that.

The Olive Branch Methodist Church formed in Perrysburg in 1843, but its congregation eventually disbanded. The Calvary Methodist Episcopal Church, the first church to be organized in Erie Township, was founded in 1846, but membership gradually dwindled away. A Methodist society formed at Miami in 1846, three years before the village was laid out. The society's membership eventually dropped, too, but the Methodist Ladies Aid Society once served hot lunches to children of the Miami School during the winter and dinners in the gymnasium to threshing crews in summer.

Methodists also met in the Bunker Hill and Converse areas at about the same time. The Converse Methodists built a church in 1855. Bunker Hill dedicated its first Methodist Church, nicknamed the "Railroad Chapel," in 1855. Waupecong's Methodist frame house of worship, built in 1854, became the first church in Clay Township. The McGrawsville Methodist congregation formed shortly thereafter. Santa Fe's congregation built a church in 1869. Denver's Methodist church

The Weasaw Creek Baptist Church congregation organized in 1840, but the first church wasn't built until 1851. The church took it name from an Indian tribe living in the area. Courtesy of the Miami County Historical Society.

The Old Friends Church, built by the Quakers in 1866 at Amboy, was abandoned after the brick church was built in 1907. The modern Friends Church was built in 1908. Courtesy of the Miami County Historical Society.

organized in 1873. Amboy's Methodist Church society formed later still.

The first Evangelical Lutheran Church services were held in 1849 in a Peru schoolhouse. Because the congregation was small, the minister visited at irregular intervals, and then discontinued visits for a year. However, the minister eventually returned and a church formally organized in 1858. The congregation grew during the 1860s. In 1855 ministers began holding services in the area of Bunker Hill. Services were held in members' homes and then in a school until a church was built.

The Presbyterian church society formed at a Peru home in 1835. About 1850 the Presbyterian church organized in Perrysburg and offered services in the school house. However, its membership gradually dwindled away. Converse's Presbyterian society, which formed in 1870, fared better. Bodurtha reported the congregation as still meeting in 1914.

The first Baptist services in Miami County possibly took place in Allen Township in 1838. In the 1840s, a Baptist minister held services in Erie Township. Though a church society organized, no church was built. However, Baptists erected a log church in Bunker

This was an early Mennonite Church in Harrison Township. The first church was built after 1855. Courtesy of the Miami County Historical Society.

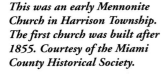

Hill. The Chili Baptist Church society formed in 1856, but services had been held in the area for some years before that.

The Mexico Baptist Church society organized in 1861. Five years later the Baptists organized a church in Peru, and an Oakdale branch of the church formed in 1905. The Denver Baptist Church society organized in 1886. Three branches of the German Baptist denomination sprang up in the county's early days—German Baptist, Church of the Brethren, and the Progressive Brethren. The first of these denominations formed in Mexico about 1837 with services held at members' homes, and in summer, at "God's first temples"—groves of trees.

The Christians, or Disciples, first established themselves in Miami around 1848. A Christian Church was built in Peoria in 1856. Bunker Hill had a society form in 1865 followed by one in Converse in 1868. The New Lights, or New Light Christians, first met in Erie Township at an early date, but formed no official society. The county's first New Light Church established itself in 1841, adopting the name Christian Salem Church. However, after a frame church was built

This was the "Calico" or "Eelpot" Church. The Methodist Church split into two congregations at one point. The "calico" congregation split with the "silk" congregation and built the Eelpot Church across from where the new Methodist Church was built at Cass and Main Streets. Courtesy of the Miami County Historical Society.

The whole congregation of the Macy Christian Church, built in 1872, seems to have turned out for this photograph. The Christian Church was organized in Macy in 1868. Courtesy of the Miami County Historical Society.

along Eel River, the congregation became known as the Eel River Church.

The United Brethren Church first formed a society in Erie Township at a home in 1849. Another society formed near Bennetts Switch in 1854, at Converse in 1856, at Waupecong in the 1880s, and at Macy in 1892. A United Brethren Church at North Grove was built in 1870. A German Evangelical Association Church was built near Gilead in 1858. Peru's church was dedicated in 1902.

Only one known Congregationalist society formed in Miami County. Many of its members had split from Peru's Presbyterian Church in 1876 along with the church's pastor, but the society eventually folded. Other early church societies that formed in Miami County include the Seventh Day Adventists, the Church of God, the Universalists, and the Christian Scientists.

This Chili Baptist Church was dedicated in 1917. Baptist ministers held services in the area long before an earlier Baptist Church was built in 1878. Courtesy of the Miami County Historical Society.

This Stringtown Church was moved to Bennetts Switch. Courtesy of Jerry Wise.

The Peoria United Methodist Church was moved in 1962 before construction of the Mississinewa dam and its resulting reservoir flooded the area. Courtesy of Betty Robison and Anna F. Wimmer.

This United Brethren Church in Deedsville still stands. Courtesy of the Miami County Historical Society.

This photograph shows the Five Corners Methodist Church which burned about 1949. The church society built its first church in 1860 about three years after the village grew into its own. The church was one of the few buildings that remained after the railroad diverted the village's trade to nearby Macy. Courtesy of the Miami County Historical Society.

Pipe Creek Brethren Church stands near where the village of Nead once stood. It once had a public school and a general store. A minister of the United Brethren Church first held services in Pipe Creek Township in a private home in the 1840s. Courtesy of the Miami County Historical Society.

This is Bunker Hill's Methodist Church. The first Methodist congregation organized in 1846 with the first services held in a little log house. Courtesy of the Miami County Historical Society.

This is the interior of St. John Lutheran Church. Courtesy of the Miami County Historical Society.

This is the interior of St. Charles Catholic Church. Courtesy of the Miami County Historical Society.

This collage shows Peru churches of various time periods. The first Catholic church was built in 1835 followed by the first Methodist and Presbyterian churches in 1836. The first Episcopal church was built after 1843, the first Christian church was dedicated in 1849, and the first Lutheran church was built after 1858. The Church of the Brethren was constructed probably sometime before 1860 while the first Baptist church was constructed in 1868. The Wayman African Methodist Episcopal Church was built in 1871. The first Wesleyan Methodist (W.M.) church was built before 1900. The first United Brethren was built in 1901 and the first Christian Science church was after 1902. Courtesy of Otis E. Marks.

This was an East End School kindergarten. The boy in black at right is future famous song composer, Cole Porter, at about age five. He was born in 1891. U.S. postal stamps, first issued in Peru, commemorated Porter on the centennial of his birth. The school stood where Davis Park stands on Peru's East Main Street today. Courtesy of the Miami County Historical Society.

CHAPTER 5

Education

Before Miami County had many schools, children often started at school at home, learning from the Bible and other available books. Educating their children followed closely on the heels of the early pioneers' desire for a place of worship. Sometimes the first churches doubled as schools, and where a school was built first, a church congregation might meet there until a church was built.

The first schools often stood on land donated by a local farmer or purchased from him. Sometimes schools took their names from the farmer or from one family. Erie Township's Long Island School was once called the Butt School because all but three students came from the Butt family. Other schools had names like Little Red Onion, Rabbit's Glory, Haystack College, Burntwoods, Buckwheat, and Mud. It is not recorded how Butler Township's Little Red Onion derived its name. However, Rabbit's Glory in Allen Township was originally called Walnut Grove until the walnut trees died. It then became known as Rabbit's Glory because of all the wildlife living in the area. Perry Township's Haystack College derived its name from a stack of hay in a corner of the schoolyard.

Richland Township's Burnt Woods School stood on the Charles Cook farm. A short time before the school was erected, a small woods covering about ten acres burned. The land burned in the shape of a rectangle with the exception of a mall indentation on one side. The surrounding community, which had been undecided as to where to build the school, agreed that it should be built in the indentation on the edge of the burned woods. At Perry Township's Pleasant Hill School, the patrons, "held literary societies, spelling schools and debates as forms of entertainments. Some of the subjects for debates were: resolved, that Columbus should have more honor for discovering America than Washington for freeing it; resolved, that capital punishment should be abolished; and resolved, that women should have the right of suffrage."

This was the first Central School in Peru with its first teachers. Built in 1860, Central stood at Sixth and Miami Streets. Central was Peru's first free public school. Courtesy of the Miami County Historical Society.

Buckwheat, built in 1886 as the third school on that location, stood three and a half miles north of Denver. The first two schools were called the Old Frame Building and the New Frame Building, but how Buckwheat got its name remains a mystery. Deer Creek Township's Mud School took its name from mud chinking between the logs and in its chimney. Also, the surrounding land hadn't been drained, so the teachers and students had to wear boots.

Logs schools had mud chinking to keep out drafts, and their fireplaces had chimneys made of mud and sticks. Oiled paper covered any windows. Parents paid a subscription, or fee, for their children to attend. The fee varied from school to school, but Miss Katie Bally, who taught at Richland Township's Port Royal in 1883, "received one dollar per pupil for a six-week term." However, some school terms ran three months out of the year. A term might begin in late fall when the children no longer had to help with harvest on the farms. The term might then end before the children were needed to help with spring planting. The children walked to school, sometimes for many miles until the county's population grew to the point where a school, which housed all grades in one or two rooms, was built about every two miles or so.

Early desks often consisted of heavy planks laid across wooden pegs with heavy wooden slabs for seats. In winter, benches inside might become sleds outside. Children also ice skated during the winter at recess if a pond stood nearby, or they might go bobsledding.

"The winter sports were fox and geese and sliding down Nicholson Hill. During the winter of 1898 the older boys built a

Among the Hockman School students in Deer Creek Township, some are at play and some pose with their teacher, Ressie (Babe) Herrell. Mrs. John Miller stands with a baby. Four Miller children—Edna, Emmet, Maine, and one identified without a first name—were listed in the picture. All three Hockman schools stood on the Hockman farm near Miami. The first was built in 1856. The third one, shown above, was built in 1876. Courtesy of Jackie J. Pearcy.

Demuth School, located six miles south of Peru, was so-called because it stood near the home of Elias Demuth. The first teacher was William Demuth Sr. The school, probably built in the 1870s, was closed in 1922 and converted to the summer home of George Demuth who became a federal inspector of commercial bee hives. Courtesy of the Miami County Historical Society.

large bobsled holding about twenty people. The Nicholson Hill was very high and steep, giving the children in the bobsled a long ride of nearly one mile in a single trip," from a school theme about California School in Erie Township, author unknown.

Telling tales of American heroes and early county pioneers counted for entertainment during cold weather. Other recess activities included games like dare base, townball, marbles, jacks, Andy-over, skip rope rhyming, blind man's bluff, and drop the handkerchief. Older boys sometimes chopped wood for the school's fireplace or stove, or they carried water to the school from a nearby farm. Parents could check on their children's progress by attending spelling bees and ciphering contests. Sometimes on the last day of school, whole families attended school and enjoyed a picnic of sorts. At Christmas, students might lock their teacher out until he promised a treat, such as a bag of candy.

Port Royal School, built in 1883, now serves as Doud Orchards' sales room along State Road 19 north of Chili. The school's bricks were hauled by horses from south of Peru. The first Port Royal School, which was built of logs, stood on Ida Doud's farm. Courtesy of the Miami County Historical Society.

Allen Township's first Birmingham School also hosted weddings and funerals. The children either went out to play or huddled in a corner until the proceedings ended, but apparently such activities didn't dampen the children's spirits. "The students of this school and period were so full of mischief that it was nicknamed 'The Wildcat College' by the people of the locality," from a school theme, author unknown.

A Mr. Hally taught Harrison Township's Stitt School in the 1880s, but according to a school theme, "No one liked him. All term he went to school but no pupils came. He put in his time, but did not have to work and got his wages." The Evans School in Peru Township sometimes had as many as four teachers in a school year. According to a school theme, "They were run out as it was termed. If a teacher came who could handle all the bullies at once and avoid a dunking in the river, he was allowed to stay one year."

Wayne McGuire wrote in his 1932 theme of a school located across from the Jefferson Township High School, "The building was a brick structure with two rooms, one upstairs and one downstairs. It was surrounded by a board fence so the livestock couldn't get close." Students at the Long Island School, built in Erie Township in 1846, saw canal boats pulled by mules pass by on the Wabash and Erie Canal.

Walking back and forth to school in early days had its hazards. Wolves killed six-year-old John Caulk on his way home from Macy School in 1840, seven years before the last wolves were killed in the county. And teacher Carrie LeVaugh walked from Macy down the railroad track to Hopewell School carrying a gun for protection against "tramps."

"After arriving at school, she loaned the revolver to the older boys so they could go down to the prairie, rabbit hunting. This kind

Denver College, founded as a private school by a German professor and a local man, W. O. Piper, was built in 1876. It closed as a college about 1878, but was used as a public school for many years. It was razed in 1912, and another school built in its place. Courtesy of the Miami County Historical Society.

Horse-drawn school hacks, probably first used in the late 1880s, were still in use nearly forty years later, but winter posed hazards for them. "Those roads would be icy and the horses could hardly make it. So they would get out and push the hack, and I would have to drive the horses," recounted Velma Mongosa Way, born in Miami County in 1912. Courtesy of the Miami County Historical Society.

Mollie O'Brian taught at the Cripe School in Pipe Creek Township. The original school, which was made of logs, gave way to a frame structure built about 1863. Courtesy of the Miami County Historical Society.

of conduct proved unsatisfactory to the patrons so the rabbit hunting was stopped," said Irene Sanders and Zadie R. Slisher, writing in their school themes.

Beginning around the 1890s, schools began to consolidate, a trend that continued through the first sixty years of this century until there exists four school corporations today—Oak Hill, Maconaquah, North Miami, and Peru.

Many of the old schools had been razed or sold for use as storage places or homes even before consolidation began. Other schools, abandoned and all but forgotten, can still be seen today, usually standing in some field. They remind us of a time when land not only provided agriculture, but often space for education. However, though rural schools gradually disappeared, agriculture continued to provide a living for county residents—then and now.

Thomas School stood in or near Bunker Hill. Note the outhouse on the left and bell tower on the roof. Courtesy of the Miami County Historical Society.

This 1891 photograph shows Butler Township's Stony Point School with Edd Bakehorn, teacher. Built in 1882 on Gabriel Godfroy's land, the school was sometimes called the Godfroy School, but eventually took its name from the many boulders in its yard. The school also served as a community center where church services and a debating society took place. One debate resolved that "chewing gum does more good than a broom," which started a discussion that "lasted for two evenings." Courtesy of the Miami County Historical Society.

These shop class students probably attended the Peru High School built, circa 1910, on the northwest corner of Sixth and Miami Streets where the Miami Indian tribal complex stands today. The Miami Nation of Indians of Indiana purchased the building in 1990. Courtesy of the Miami County Historical Society.

These students, identified only as Creta, Estelle, Bessie, and Eleanor, were photographed in Peru High School's chemistry lab, circa 1899. Peru's first high school was built in 1834 as a log building. Later, high school classes occupied a former livery barn at the southwest corner of Sixth and Broadway. Courtesy of the Miami County Historical Society.

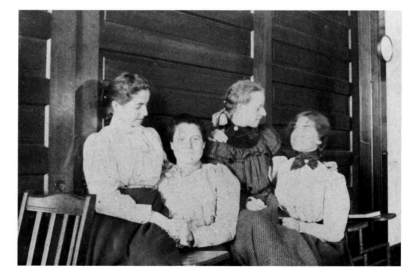

Ridgeview School was named for the village which once adjoined Peru's city limits. Built on a hill next to Mount Hope Cemetery in 1910, the school didn't have electric lights until about 1914. It was closed about 1974 and razed in 1977. Courtesy of the Miami County Historical Society.

The old St. Lutheran School opened on West Second Street in 1905. It is now a private residence. Courtesy of the Miami County Historical Society.

St. Charles Parochial School, made possible by a contribution from the widow of local circus magnate, Jerry Mugivan, was dedicated in 1931. Among the guest speakers was the president of Notre Dame University, A. Harvey Cole. Courtesy of the Miami County Historical Society.

Drum major Bob Dye stands ready to lead the Clay Township High School marching band. The school was built about 1923. Courtesy of the Miami County Historical Society.

Students present a play at Chili High School in the 1950s. Note the old style school desks that were still in use. The 1959 junior class presented No More Homework, *a play based on a factual newspaper account of what happened when circumstances forced three high school students to become principal, vice principal, and secretary in a typical high school of the time. Chili's old frame high school stood across from the Methodist Church. The brick high school was built in 1917. Courtesy of the Miami County Historical Society.*

All of Butler Township School's students turned out for this photograph. The school, located near Peoria, was built about 1915 and closed sometime in the 1960s after schools were consolidated and the Maconaquah School Corporation formed. Butler's basketball team, the "Tomahawks," won the county tournament in 1934. An old barn was converted to the school's gymnasium. Two potbellied stoves heated it, but students had to cross an open field to reach the showers in the school. The school was eventually razed. Courtesy of the Miami County Historical Society.

Friends and neighbors threshed grain on the Philip Smith homestead, circa 1916. The building behind the wagon, right, was Quarrel Hill School, built before 1853 and later called Shilow. It was moved from the Allen Smith woods to the homestead. Courtesy of Barbara J. Amiss.

CHAPTER 6

Agriculture

"I've showed in all forty-eight states, and if I was going to spend any money on farms, it would be in Miami County. I would rather invest my money in Wabash Valley black bottom land than Wall Street," reported Ben Wallace, founder of Peru's own circus and circus winter quarters in 1913.

Wallace did indeed invest in Miami County farms where he raised crops to feed some of his circus animals. Always interested in circuses and menageries, Wallace first established his circus winter quarters in 1881 where Poor Farm Country Candies now stands along Indiana 124 east of Peru. He then eventually bought, westward toward Peru, Wallcourt Farm—which no longer stands—on the north side of 124, Fairview on the south side, Hillcrest next to the present circus winter quarters on the north, the winter quarters itself, and Springdale on the south. Wallace's wife lived at Springdale up on the hill where she maintained an exotic garden with plants from all over the world. Wallace had an entrance gate

Pearl and Arthur Lewis plowed corn on their Bunker Hill farm in this 1924 photograph. Courtesy of Paul Lewis.

for each of his farms, each gate bearing the farm's name, gold leaf, and hand-carving. White board fence stretched along both sides of the road running by the farms. The barns were painted yellow, Wallace's favorite color.

In 1891 Wallace bought today's circus winter quarters, located along the Mississinewa River, from Gabriel Godfroy, son of the last Miami war chief, Francis Godfroy.

Francis Godfroy already lived on Butler Township's "black bottom land" in a home which he used also as a trading post when Martin Wilhelm was reportedly the first white man to settle within the future township's limits in 1839. Other pioneers moved into the area and into Miami County to

Daniel Duckwall, who settled in Pipe Creek Township after 1847, built this barn, one of the first bank barns in Miami County. Such barns had a "bank" of earth that sloped up to the barn's doors on one side so that wagons and other equipment could enter the barn's second level. Livestock could enter the lower level directly from the other side of the barn. Some bank barns still stand in the county today. Courtesy of the Miami County Historical Society.

homestead farms until by the mid-1850s, they formed a Miami County Agricultural Society. A fairground was then set up a short distance from Peru on the William Smith farm. According to Bodurtha's history, " . . . old settlers remember that the fairs were well attended, as a rule, and did a great deal of good in stimulating a spirit of friendly emulation among the farmers of the county, many of who tried every year to make a better showing of field products and livestock than their neighbors."

The society eventually disbanded, but the Xenia Union Agricultural Society formed in 1871. Land was leased on which to stage the fair which first opened in September 1871. Such was the fair's success that buildings and a race track were then constructed.

The Peru Driving Park and Fair Association incorporated in 1873, but gradually interest in it and its fairs waned. Then in 1884 the Macy Fair Association formed. A land tract was bought on which to host the fair about two and a half miles north of the town. The location proved to be too small, however, so twenty acres were purchased west of Macy where buildings and a half mile race track were built. Still, fair attendance was not as large as expected and debt piled up for the association until it liquidated its assets in 1896. The Miami County Driving Park and Agricultural Society, formed in 1890 " . . . to encourage mechanical, manufacturing, and scientific enterprises, and the care, training, and breeding of livestock," leased Macy's fairgrounds in 1890 and 1891. As for a fair association, another one did not form until 1908 when the Miami County Agricultural Association organized at Converse.

Meanwhile, farmers had their barns raised by dozens of friends and neighbors just as pioneer ancestors together raised log cabins.

This was the Smith homestead, circa 1875, which has been in the Smith family over one hundred years. Note the split rail and board fences. A brick house was built on the farm in 1887. The original owner, Philip Smith, was a German emigrant. Courtesy of Barbara J. Amiss.

This combination cider mill, sorghum mill, and jelly factory, circa 1897, stood on Henry Moseley's farm on the west side of Strawtown Pike about four and a half miles south of Peru. Moseley was also the first breeder of purebred short horn Durham cattle south of the Wabash River in Miami County. Courtesy of the Louanna Wilson Estate.

A crowd of people posed outside New Santa Fe's elevator in the early 1900s. When New Santa Fe became a station on the Chesapeake and Ohio Railroad, the elevator was built to handle the extra business. Courtesy of the Miami County Historical Society.

Groups of farmers in an area would gather to thresh each other's grain in turns while their families gathered to prepare meals for the threshing crews. Wallace constructed a complex of barns and training arenas that would eventually encompass twenty acres on his winter quarters while his farms, which included around twenty-seven hundred acres, produced hay, corn, and oats with draft horse power. Horses that became too old to work or perform in the circus, were killed and fed to the tigers, lions, and other large cats. Sometimes local farmers sold their aging horses to the circus for the same purpose, or traded them for circus horses too old to perform, but healthy enough yet to pull a wagon or carry a rider.

Other farmers raised corn, oats, and hay, too, along with wheat, rye, tomatoes, potatoes, and more. Bodurtha reported that the 1911 berry and other fruit crops had increased over those of the year before, bearing out a statement of the time that "the possibilities of fruit raising on a commercial scale are just beginning to be realized." Also in 1911, Miami County farmers raised 39,256 hogs compared to

5,392 head of cattle, with "considerable attention given to dairying."

Several county farm producers achieved moments in the agricultural spotlight. Joseph Cunningham had the distinction of becoming the Indiana State Swine Association's president in 1893. In 1903 Linc Lukens and Reahard and Ohmart sold "Ideal Sunrise," a Poland China hog, for $15,812.50 at a Macy swine sale. "Majestic Perfection" sold for $8,800 and "Majestic Perfection II" sold for $6,200. Over two hundred hogs were entered in the auction with sales amounting to over $55,000. George E. Moseley and his son, Edwin, turned from raising Poland Chinas and Chesters to purebred Duroc swine in 1901. They staged Duroc sales from 1902 up through the 1940s.

Bodurtha reported John Miller of Jefferson Township as having "taken more prizes at world and state fairs and other livestock exhibits than any cattleman in Indiana. Mrs. Miller has two or more bed quilts made of ribbons awarded her husband in these stock shows—most of them representing first prizes—and the supply of ribbons was not then exhausted. Mr. Miller has sold cattle all over the county and even to breeders in South America." Another prominent cattle raiser, Clem Garves of Pipe Creek Township, once sold "a single Here-

This 1908 photograph depicts the delivery of International Reapers by the Farmer's Hardware of Amboy. Amboy also had a creamery which served approximately four thousand farmers until farmers began separating their milk at home and feeding the whey to livestock. Courtesy of Jackie J. Pearcy.

An open air farmers' market behind Peru's courthouse is shown here around turn of the century. Note the women with their shopping baskets and the policeman strolling beside the woman with a baby in her arms. Courtesy of the Miami County Historical Society.

ford bull for the handsome sum of $10,000."

Other farm producers have received recognition through the Hoosier Homestead Award for keeping their farms in the same family a century or more. As of 1994, forty-two Miami County families had received the award since the Indiana Office of Commissioner of Agriculture began offering it in the 1970s. At one time four of Miami County's Hoosier Homestead farms had been in the same family at least one hundred fifty years. Among those that remain is Doud Orchards.

In 1994 Noel and Marsha Hunt of Amboy became the forty-second Miami County family to receive the Hoosier Homestead Award. About 1867, John A. Lamb helped lay out Amboy as a station on the new Pan Handle Railroad. In 1871 B. B. Lamb laid out an addition to the town. And in 1886 Sarah Lamb Hunt obtained a twenty-acre farm near the town. One hundred and eight years later, those same twenty acres—and more—belong to Sarah's great-grandson, Noel. "If you look around the neighborhood, having a farm in the same family one hundred years is not real common . . . You have to love farming to be out here," said Noel Hunt on receiving the Hoosier Homestead Award.

Today, county farmers produce mostly corn, soybeans, and in terms of livestock—hogs. Farms have dwindled in number, but grown generally larger. They still provide a living for many residents, but today people often identify more closely with business and industry than with their agricultural roots. In the past, though, business and industry followed agriculture in expanding Miami County's horizons. But to keep those horizons organized as they expanded, government developed. And military groups developed in response to the needs of a nation beyond those horizons.

Miami County Corn Club members gathered in front of Peru's courthouse in the early 1900s. In 1931 thousands of people gathered at James Tinkcom's Peru farm on Frances Slocum Trail for the state corn husking contest. Courtesy of the Miami County Historical Society.

Old Ben, a shorthorn Hereford cross born on the Mike Murphy farm in 1902, may have been about the largest steer in the world when destroyed in 1910. He weighed 135 pounds at birth and forty-seven hundred pounds at his death with a length of sixteen feet two inches and a height of six feet four inches. He was shown at state and county fairs for many years until he broke his leg after falling on a patch of ice. Marion Stonerock of Miami butchered Ben, and a local grocer wanted the beef, but local women threatened to boycott the store. An Indianapolis frankfurter company eventually bought the beef. Ben's hide was stuffed and mounted for display at the Murphy farm until 1919 when it was donated to Kokomo where it is now displayed at Highland Park. Courtesy of the Miami County Historical Society.

This twelve-sided barn, built by Mark Borden in 1912 and razed in 1981, stood in Washington Township and had rectangular additions to it. The site was one of six Miami County round barn sites listed by John Hanou in his 1993 book, A Round Indiana. *Three more round barn sites have been confirmed in the county since Hanou's book was published. One such barn, which stood on land belonging to Doyne E. Guy on State Road 218 west of U.S. 31, was discovered while researching material for this book. The Guy barn was razed in 1942 to make way for Bunker Hill Naval Air Base which later became Grissom Air Force Base, now Grissom Aeroplex. Two round barns still stand in the county. Courtesy of Ralph Clymer.*

This 1913 photo shows Wahlig's Dairy delivery in front of the Miller residence on Bobtail Pike. Peru also had Gilt Edge, Quality, and William Liebo Dairies. Bunker Hill had Betzner's Jersey Dairy, Converse had Hodson Dairy, and Macy had Smith's Dairy. Amboy had Yoars Dairy, Denver had Shoemaker's Dairy, and Mexico had Modern Dairy. Courtesy of the Miami County Historical Society.

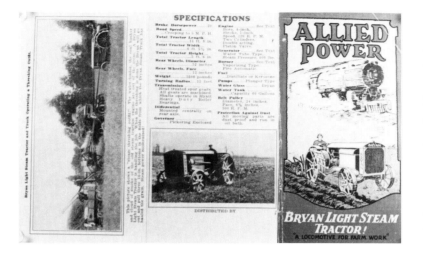

Bryan Harvester Company came from New Mexico to Peru around 1918 where it produced a steam tractor and car. The Peru Republican reported that five thousand people in Peru watched the Bryan tractor perform a special demonstration on 1924, before it went on tour. However, gasoline soon replaced steam for powering tractors and cars, but the newly named Bryan Steam Corporation stayed in business and operates in Peru today. Courtesy of the Miami County Historical Society.

This threshing crew appears dwarfed by a "mountain" of grain it has already harvested. Threshing crews sometimes traveled from state to state seeking work. Courtesy of the Miami County Historical Society.

This 1926 photograph shows the Sharp and Overman Company at McGrawsville. In the background, right, stands the elevator, which was built in 1903. From left to right are: Jim Fiser, Raymond Shively, John Reminger, Alvin Powell (elevator man), elevator owner, Ralph Overman, Dorothea Overman, Vera Weaver (store clerk), and the store owner, Charles Sharp. Courtesy of Rhonda Blackburn.

Top photo: The old Miami County fairgrounds with a track for horse racing which was possibly located near the Wabash River west of Peru at about where the city limits are now. The Peru Driving Park and Fair Association incorporated in 1873 "to promote the agricultural, horticultural, mechanical, and household interests of the county," according to Bodurtha's history. Interest in the fairs waned by 1884, however, and they were no longer held there. Miami County's 4-H Fair was eventually opened in West City Park, which was established after 1902 and originally named Reyburn Park after the farming family whose land it stood on. Today's county fairgrounds, which opened in 1954, stands just north of Peru along old U.S. 31. Courtesy of the Miami County Historical Society.

The Peru Fruit Company stood north of the railroad underpass over Broadway in 1923. Today the site is the parking lot next to Hardee's restaurant. From left to right are: Ray Douglas, an unknown boy, Angie (last name unknown), an unknown girl, Vida Ferree, Frank Russo, and two unidentified boys. Courtesy of the Miami County Historical Society.

Facing page: George Demuth, a prominent local beekeeper, posed with his beehives. He later became state inspector of commercial beehives, then federal inspector and lived in Washington, D.C. part of the year. Courtesy of the Miami County Historical Society.

Top right: Rex Gilbreath, seated on the tractor, and a B. F. Goodrich representative are shown in this 1935 photograph taken on the Ira Gilbreath farm. The tractor was the first one with rubber tires in Miami County. Courtesy of the Miami County Historical Society.

Bottom right: The 1943 flood reached Sullivan's Hatchery at 110 South Broadway. Note the patriotic slogan "Idle Brooders Help the Enemy." Courtesy of the Miami County Historical Society.

Below: Grant Zook once made maple sugar. He and his wife, Vera, owned the sugar camp on State Road 218 east of Bunker Hill from 1946 until 1957. Only a handful of sugar camps exist in the county today. In 1918 the Peru Republican *reported that local resident Frank Ward urged sugar maple production to overcome the sugar shortage caused by World War I. Courtesy of Grant and Vera Zook.*

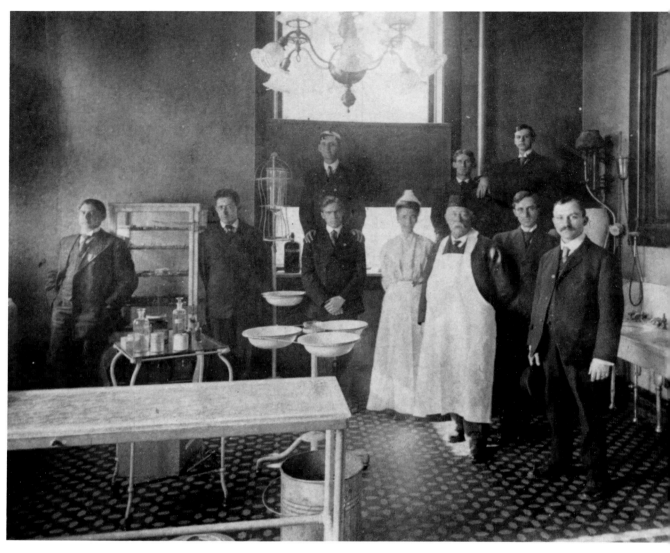

This was the operating room of Dukes Memorial Hospital, circa 1915. From left to right are: L. Jennett;
R. A. Poak; ambulance driver Bert Marshall (back); C. S. Houty (front); Miss Helen McDougal;
O. R. Lynch (back); the pharmacist, a Mr. Keeman (in apron); Tracy Earhart (back); and a Mr. Mulheny.
The man on the far right was not identified. Dukes, named for Captain Aaron Dukes who broke ground
for the hospital, opened without proper beds in time to receive victims of the 1913 flood. A Miami County
Medical Society formed earlier in 1875. Courtesy of the Miami County Historical Society.

CHAPTER 7

Government and Military

Miami County's first military company, the "Peru Blues," organized in 1836 and was called out at least once when it was reported the Potawatomi Indians had risen against the government in adjoining Fulton County. Between forty and fifty members of the "Blues" assembled, fully equipped and armed. The expedition then marched out over the Mexico Road, and as a "war measure," pressed into service any horses along the line of march. However, there was no uprising and the company returned home shortly.

However, there did exist problems with horse thieves. During the 1830s and 1840s, gangs of horse thieves organized in Indiana and nearby states. One such gang established a headquarters "a mile or so west of Gilead," but the gang could never be caught there, because, it was believed, "a lookout was kept in some tree top." The gang, which later linked up with counterfeiters, was eventually infiltrated by a detective who helped catch some of the criminals. However, it took a vigilance committee which had authority to arrest "any suspicious character" to convince the thieves to depart the area.

This 1848 certificate confirmed Eben Moseley as postmaster of Palos. Palos does not appear on any known maps. However, post offices of the time were often located in a general store or even the postmaster's house. Research indicates Palos probably included the area of the Moseley farm along Strawtown Pike. Courtesy of the Miami County Historical Society.

Miami County had no American flag for the 1844 July Fourth celebration, so "young men agreed to buy the material if the young women would make a flag." The flag first flew, with stars representing twenty-four states, on July 4, 1844, "in a grove near the corner of Seventh and Hood Streets." The drum was played at the opening of the Wabash and Erie Canal and during the Mexican civil war. Courtesy of the Miami County Historical Society.

In terms of government, Peru's town board formed in 1842 with Peru incorporating in 1848. At that time the marshal was instructed to locate the town's fire ladders. These ladders were to be kept in the "most suitable place," but they were usually left at the scene of the last fire which raised some difficulty in remembering where they were. Later, around 1860, a volunteer fire department organized. A year after that, volunteers were needed for war.

President Lincoln's call for volunteers to fight against the South reached Peru on April 16, 1861, the day of William H. Shields' birthday. He and about one hundred men volunteered and were inducted into Company B of the Thirteenth Regiment of Indiana Infantry. In 1862 Shields became captain of his company, a rank he held until severely wounded and sent home. He lived in Peru until 1866 when he learned a regiment of cavalry was forming to fight the Indians on the Great Plains under the command of a young Civil War hero— George Armstrong Custer. Shields enlisted for three years in Company 4, Seventh U.S. Cavalry, and in doing so, became a charter

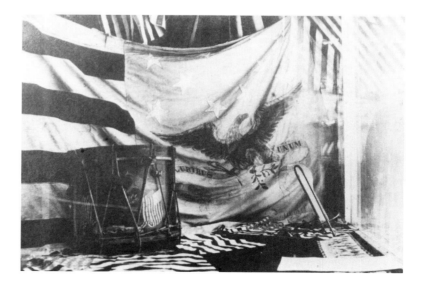

member of the force that became a legend. Shields was in Captain Frederick Benteen's pack train, separated that fateful day from Custer and his men who died at the Battle of Little Big Horn. Benteen, Shields, and others topped a bluff and saw eighteen hundred Sioux lodges plus a herd of Indian ponies so numerous "the hills had an odd, reddish brown color." Shields survived the attack by the Sioux that followed, but he never returned to Peru. He died some years later and was buried in the Indian Territory that later became Oklahoma.

Bodurtha reported that during the Civil War, Miami County was one of the "few counties in the state" where "not a single citizen . . . left his home to avoid the draft." However, there existed Southern sympathizers, such as the Knights of the Golden Circle who held secret meetings in Clay Township's Studebaker School and other places. In later years, though, Miami County hosted more public political meetings.

County Republicans entertained James G. Blaine, Republican presidential candidate, at Peru, along with several other leading Indiana Republicans in 1884. Newspapers of the time reported the meeting as "one of the greatest rallies ever given by any party in Miami County." Not to be outdone, the Democrats hosted a barbecue two days after the Republicans' meeting. Democratic vice presidential candidate Thomas A. Hendricks attended, as did thousands of supporters. In the evening there followed fireworks and parade with "1,025 torches in line and a very large drunk."

Temperance movements, like the Sons of Temperance and the Independent Order of the Good Templars, were in the news also. The Anti-Liquor League, founded about 1893, asked its members to "support and vote only for those candidates for public office whose opinions, habits, associations and past record are a satisfactory guarantee

These were Civil War veterans. From left to right, back row, are: Sergeant A. A. Ream, Company Clerk Gus Bradferd, and Sergeant Ed Smith. From left to right, front row, are: Captain Meyers, Sergeant Ben Toggert, and Lieutenant McDaniel. Courtesy of the Miami County Historical Society.

Former President Benjamin Harrison, standing next to the flag, visited Peru as a guest of the Republicans in the 1890s. He served as president from 1889 to 1892. Courtesy of the Miami County Historical Society.

President William McKinley stopped in Peru while on the campaign trail. He served as president from 1897 to 1901. Courtesy of the Miami County Historical Society.

that they are free from the influence of liquor forever . . ." (Bodurtha). In 1900 the *Peru Republican* reported that "Andy Oliver's saloon in Macy was visited by a group of women who held prayer service." Nine years later, county residents voted to go "dry" in a special county election.

The two World Wars touched Miami County residents' lives in more ways than one. During World War I in 1917, Miami County not only sent men to fight, but organized its farmers for greater food production to meet war needs at the request of Indiana Governor James Goodrich. And when the war ended in November 1918, schoolchildren and their teachers marched through the streets singing "Over There," with each child waving a flag.

By World War II, Miami County not only sent men to fight and raised food to feed them, but manufactured products for the war effort. Private William Brenton, wounded in 1944 on the Italian front, was reported by the *Peru Republican* as "receiving a thrill" whenever he looked down into an American tank and read the label "Sherrill Research Corporation, Peru, Indiana" on the compass. After recovering from his wound, Brenton went to work at Sherrill which stood on the east side of the courthouse square and also maintained a factory in Mexico. "I hope I am handling the compass that directs the way to Berlin and Hitler. I know what war is; I won't let the boys down . . . I can no longer be with the guys on the battle front, but I can still help them by working on the home front," he was quoted as saying, February 28, 1944.

Beginning in 1945 Oglesby Manufacturing in Peru produced aluminum toy cars followed by jeeps and other toys that have since become collectors' items. Before that time, Thomas W. Oglesby and his father, George, owned a factory on Adams Avenue that produced many things for America's war effort. Among them were bomb bay door rollers for the big bomber planes. Then two FBI agents from Bunker Hill Naval Station showed up at Oglesby Manufacturing one day with an order marked "Top Secret - Manhattan Project" across the top. The agents told him to work on the project day and night to complete it. Then it was to be handed to the agents only if they came together. Thomas, who recognized the project as a timing device, finished it in forty-eight hours. "He didn't find out until the general public knew that the Manhattan Project was synonymous with the atomic bomb dropped on Hiroshima and Nagasaki," said Bill Oglesby, speaking of his father, Thomas.

Peru's volunteer fire department got its own building in 1888 on Miami Street which still stands today. A paid fire department was established in 1889, and the last fire horses were used between 1915 and 1918. Courtesy of the Miami County Historical Society.

Members of the Miami County Horse Thief Association, formed in 1900 by Miami County Sheriff John Volpert, gathered for a picnic. In 1905 Volpert organized the State Police, Sheriffs, Marshals, and Detectives Association, today known as the National Sheriffs Association. Over three hundred members from around Indiana gathered in Peru for the association's first meeting. Courtesy of the Miami County Historical Society.

The Peru Public Library was built with county funds and twenty-five thousand dollars from steel magnate Andrew Carnegie. Built in 1902, it is one of the few remaining Carnegie libraries in the country. The Peru Lyceum, organized in 1837, established a collection of early library books. Courtesy of the Miami County Historical Society.

The county's second courthouse had already been torn down and replaced when Mayor John Kreutzer ordered Sheriff John Volpert to remove hitchracks from the public square in 1910. Courtesy of the Miami County Historical Society.

This is a closeup of the second courthouse. Note the white board fence. Courtesy of the Louanna Wilson Estate.

Colonel Hiram I. Bearss, uniformed, posed in front of the home of his father, Frank Bearss, in Ridgeview. Bearss received eight decorations for valor. Among his decorations were the Legion of Honor, Croix de Guerre, Distinguished Service Cross, an award from Italy, and one from Belgium. President Franklin D. Roosevelt decorated him with the Congressional Medal of Honor for heroism in the Philippines in 1901. During World War I, Bearss once requested leave and was promised one if he would capture a German. "He took a dozen men on a raiding party that same night," a local newspaper recounted, "and came back with eighty prisoners. Bearss and his men got their leave." Courtesy of the Miami County Historical Society.

Top photo: This was Peru's old post office at the northeast corner of Sixth Street and Broadway during the 1913 flood. It was torn down and the current one built at Second Street and Broadway. Courtesy of the Miami County Historical Society.

People raised this World War I victory garden near Peru. During the war, people were encouraged to grow their own food to save canned and other foods for troops at the front. Courtesy of the Miami County Historical Society.

A Peru street crew work on a Tippecanoe Street sewer section over sixteen feet below street level in 1917. Courtesy of the Miami County Historical Society.

Facing page top: William Rennaker, center front in uniform, was reported to be Miami County's last living Civil War veteran when this photograph was taken on May 30, 1939, at Converse. Behind Rennaker on the left stands Dr. John H. Stone of Kokomo, president of the Indiana Department of the G.A.R. Behind Rennaker on the right stands Judge Hal Phelps of Peru. Phelps helped establish the Miami County Historical Society in 1916. It was said Phelps "searched attics, outbuildings, and cellars . . . and if he found anything of historical significance, the owner knew no peace until the item was safely stored in the courthouse museum." Courtesy of the Miami County Historical Society.

Facing page bottom: A Works Progress Administration street crew posed for this 1937 photograph. The WPA, a New Deal program, provided work for America's jobless during the Depression years. Between 1935 and 1942, the WPA employed an average 2.1 million persons. Courtesy of the Miami County Historical Society.

Right: Miami County native Major General William Kepner enlisted in the Marines, then in the Army and served with distinction in World War I. Afterward, he enlisted in the Air Corps and participated in history-making aircraft developments. In 1934 Kepner piloted The Explorer, *reportedly the largest freeflight balloon ever constructed. He received the Distinguished Service Cross and Distinguished Flying Cross during World War II and headed the Air Force's newly established Atomic Energy Division in 1947. Courtesy of the Miami County Historical Society.*

MAJOR W. E. KEPNER

GREETINGS FROM
MIAMI, INDIANA
∞
Best Wishes for a
Safe Journey
and a
Happy Landing.

MAJOR W. E. KEPNER,

STRATA CAMP,

RAPID CITY,

SOUTH DAKOTA

Left: This photograph shows some of the first airplanes and an outhouse at Bunker Hill Naval Air Station which opened in 1942 to train naval pilots. The base was nicknamed U.S.S. Cornfield *because that's what the land originally was. World War I aviator Lieutenant Commander Edwin Dixon, a stunt flyer in the movies* Wings, Lilac Time, Hell's Angels, *and* Dawn Patrol, *became superintendent of aviation training. The station, deactivated in 1946, was used for storage by the Air Force which reactivated the station as Bunker Hill Air Force Base in 1955. In 1968 it was renamed Grissom Air Force Base to honor Hoosier astronaut Lieutenant Colonel Virgil Grissom, one of three astronauts killed in the first fatal U.S. space program accident. The base was realigned in 1994 from active to reserve duty and renamed Grissom Aeroplex. Courtesy of the Miami County Historical Society.*

Above left: Ethel Cunningham, a teacher in Manilla, and about three thousand other Americans became prisoners of war when Japanese troops overran the Philippines during World War II. The prisoners were freed in 1945. The only inkling the prisoners had that freedom was coming was the demolition work carried out by the Japanese. Later American tanks smashed their way through the compound's walls. "Had we been told at the time of our internment that we would be confined there for more than three years, the majority of us couldn't have stood up under the treatment," said Ethel Cunningham, a prisoner of war. Courtesy of the Miami County Historical Society.

Above right: Army Private Martin F. Roop received a World War II Victory Medal during Miami County Armistice Day ceremonies in 1945. Carl Mills, who represented the Navy, also received a Victory Medal. They were the first such medals to be awarded in Miami County. Courtesy of Martin Roop.

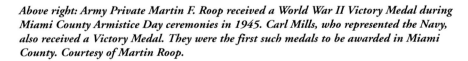

Rear Admiral Richard "Lance" Nott Antrim graduated from Peru High School and the United States Naval Academy. During World War II, he received the Navy Cross for his action during the Battle of the Java Sea, and a citation and a bronze medal from Queen Wilhelmina of the Netherlands for "unusual courage and efficiency in various encounters with the Japanese in defense of the Netherlands' East Indies." Antrim received the Congressional Medal of Honor for "defending a naval officer subjected to a clubbing by a Japanese guard while both were prisoners in Borneo." Courtesy of the Miami County Historical Society.

Louis Nelp established his meat market in Peru in 1872, buying and killing livestock himself. He sold "fresh, salt and smoked meats, delicacies in brains, sweet bread, butter, eggs, and produce, also fish, oysters, and game in season," from A Description of the City of Peru, *published in 1872. Courtesy of Jerry Wise.*

CHAPTER 8

Business and Industry

It began with trading posts, taverns and hotels, sawmills, grain mills, and blacksmiths and continued through grain elevators, breweries, woolen mills, sewing machine and phone booth factories, pianos, steam tractors, horseless carriages, and more. It is business and industry, old and new, large and small.

Among Allen Township's earliest businesses were an ashery, which supplied much of the soda used by pioneers, and the manufacture of brick. In Butler Township, the government built a mill east of Chief Godfroy's trading post in 1826. The mill, built according to treaty provisions, was to grind corn for the Miamis. A sawmill was built at Peoria, and sawmill and gristmills were built near Santa Fe. Clay Township had several sawmills and a brick yard early on. One early settler chiefly made his living by "hunting and selling whisky surreptitiously to his neighbors and the few

Oil was first struck in Peru in 1897 on land "just north of the end of Miami Street and near the Boulevard." By 1898 two hundred thirty wells had been drilled, most along either side of Grant Street. Newspaper correspondents from many metropolitan dailies wrote glowing accounts of Peru's oil fields while visitors crowded local hotels and restaurants. Oil City Hotel and Restaurant, located at 21 West Second Street, opened shortly after the oil boom started. Courtesy of the Miami County Historical Society.

Indians that remained in the locality." Later, the manufacturing of drain tile remained important until the land was drained.

Deer Creek Township had a "corn cracker" mill, and a sawmill and flour mill at Miami. Erie Township had a trading post, blacksmith, and sawmill. Harrison Township had its share of grist and sawmills, a tannery, and a blacksmith. Indians hunted on, and hunters and trappers made a living from, the Miamis' Big Reserve which later formed Jackson Township. Jefferson and Perry Townships had sawmills and trading posts. Pipe Creek Township had similar businesses along with a lime kiln and an early distillery for a time. In Richland Township, there existed gristmills, sawmills, and a flour mill. Union Township had sawmills and gristmills like Washington Township, but the latter had some of the most fertile farmland, and those early farmers living along Big Pipe Creek were referred to as "swamp angels."

Peru Township naturally witnessed the growth of the most business and industry with Peru being the county seat and located along the canal. In the late 1800s the availability of trees for wood products drew a number of industries to the township. The biggest asset to Peru's business and industry, though, was the annexation of Oakdale.

The Peru Commercial Club, established in 1902, helped push the sale of lots after the Oakdale Improvement Company filed a plat for the Oakdale addition to Peru in 1906. Among the businesses that eventually came to Peru and located in Oakdale shortly thereafter were the Mallmann Addograph, Kendalville Furniture, and Parkhurst Elevator Manufacturing Companies. The Fox Brothers underwear and Chute and Butler Piano factories also located there. But the Peru Commercial Club didn't stop with its success in Oakdale. It grew to include one hundred fifty members by 1914 and in 1922 adopted the slogan, "Try Peru first." About ten years earlier, the Amboy Civic and Industrial Club organized "to upbuild in every way [and] condition in and around Amboy and to conduct meetings wherein propositions of value to the community are to be generally discussed."

The discovery of natural gas attracted businesses in different parts of the county. The Amboy Gas and Oil Company, organized in 1887, reportedly drilled the county's first successful gas well. The Xenia Gas and Pipe Line Company, incorporated in 1887, drew businesses like the Xenia Hoop Works, Hoosier Canning Company, the Peerless Glass Company, and a carriage company. The Citizens Gas and Pipe Line Company organized in Peru in 1887. Businesses like Miami Flint Glass Works, Standard Cabinet Manufacturing Company, and others opened in Peru.

In his history, Bodurtha listed many businesses and the number of employees. Among them were Hagenbeck-Wallace Shows with five hundred people and Moeck and Redmon Basket Company with fifty-eight. He also noted that "a number of miscellaneous small concerns employed in the aggregate about 100 or more." Today the Hagenbeck-Wallace circus no longer exists, but the circus heritage it left behind at the circus winter quarters and for Peru's amateur circus draws tourists into Miami County. Redmon Basket Factory still employs people, and a number of county residents have opened "miscellaneous small concerns" which employ other residents and strive to keep people shopping "Peru first."

J. O. Cole, center in coat and vest, owned thr Peru Brewery. The brewery's wagon in an 1884 parade commemorating Peru's first Democratic barbecue carried a vat with employees "mixing the real stuff." Free beer samples, tapped from kegs on the wagon, were given out along the parade route. The brewery stood against the hill across from where Mace Food Store is today. The brewery closed when the county voted to go "dry," but the spring water used to make the beer still trickles today. Courtesy of the Miami County Historical Society.

103

This was Aley's sawmill at Weasaw in northern Miami County. Courtesy of the Miami County Historical Society.

Joseph Bergman owned and operated Bergman's Saloon in the 1890s. It stood between the Blue Drug Store and the Roxy Theater on Broadway. Note the iron stove and spittoons on the floor. Courtesy of the Miami County Historical Society.

Mexico Manufacturing Company, shown here floating down the flooded Eel River in 1904, was founded in 1876. It produced all kinds of furniture, but its business had largely faded away by 1900. Courtesy of the Miami County Historical Society.

The Schmoll brothers replaced this building with a new one for their groceries at Broadway and Fifth Street before 1900. "A full line is carried including all kinds of groceries, canned, and bottled goods, fine teas, coffees, spices, fruits, vegetables, etc. . . . In the rear is an elegantly fitted sample room, the stock of which comprises foreign and domestic wines, liquors and cigars, also fresh beer on tap at all times," from A Description of the City of Peru, published 1897. Courtesy of the Miami County Historical Society.

These men cut ice on the Eel River to keep food and drinks cool. Folklore suggests that Eel River derived its name from a Miami word meaning "snake fish," a word early settlers may have translated as "eel." Courtesy of Jerry Wise.

American Stationery, founded in 1912, was listed as one of Miami County's top ten employers in 1993. Courtesy of the Miami County Historical Society.

Top photo: Peru Wholesale Grocery Company, whose interior is shown here from the early 1900s, was organized in 1912. Fannie Becker Crune is seated in the center with John J. Kreutzer behind her. The other people were not identified. Courtesy of the Miami County Historical Society.

Rufus Kinzie, left, owned a Mexico hardware store, circa 1915.
Kinzie was a farmer and auctioneer. Courtesy of Delma E. Scott.

Top photo: The Miami Vulcanizing Company, open from 1913 to 1916, stood on
East Sixth Street. From left to right are: Esten E. Abbott, an unidentified man, and
Abbott's partner, George Petrie. Courtesy of the Miami County Historical Society.

Below: This was the interior of McCaffrey and Company with three unidentified employees. McCaffrey opened a store next to Senger Dry Goods Company around 1907. Courtesy of the Miami County Historical Society.

Senger Dry Goods Company employees received change in boxes that moved along wires from an office balcony overlooking the first floor. Senger opened at Fifth and Broadway in 1906 and closed in 1978. It opened in 1983 as the Miami County Museum, having been named a state and national historical site. "I remember going upstairs because my first formal came from Senger's. I got all my shoes there, and I think Mother bought most of my clothes there. But what I remember best is how accommodating people were there," recalled Norma Richardson, a museum volunteer. Courtesy of Darren Crowe and Helena Moore.

This basket factory, shown behind employees of the 1920s, was located in Denver's old Westlyn Church and began operating sometime before 1915. Only three employees were named in the photograph: Cleve Ege, Fred Cover, and "Hank" Cover. Courtesy of the Miami County Historical Society.

This photograph, circa 1916, shows employees inside the Model Gas Engine Company, one of many businesses that opened in the Oakdale commercial addition to Peru. The company made "noiseless engines" for Great Western Automobile Works. Courtesy of Paul Lewis.

An unidentified Wolf's Coal and Transfer Company employee, a coal salesman, and Harry Wolf, right, stand in front of the business on West Second Street. Built in 1929, part of the "coal house" still stands today. Courtesy of the Miami County Historical Society.

Converse Canning Factory employees stand outside the business in this photograph, circa 1937. Courtesy of the Miami County Historical Society.

The Royal Lunch Cafe stood on East Fifth Street behind Senger's Dry Goods Company. Pictured left to right are William "Scottie" Scott, Elsie Scott, Mary Scott, Bessie Marks, and two unidentified women. The Scotts sold the cafe in the 1940s and became manager and cook at the Red Coach Inn in the Bearss Hotel. Courtesy of Etna Wade.

Orby Bryant, holding jars of pickles, and unidentified employees stand outside Bryant's pickle factory in Macy in the 1930s. Courtesy of the Miami County Historical Society.

This was the interior of Fasnacht Jewelry Store at 65 South Broadway in 1946. Ed Fasnacht opened the store some years earlier. Courtesy of the Miami County Historical Society.

Carl J. Stengel stood at the entrance to his shoe repair service on 11 West Third Street in this photograph, circa 1960s. Courtesy of the Miami County Historical Society.

Arthur J. "Dutch" Bergman, wearing the number "3" jersey, was born in Peru in 1895 and played under Knute Rockne at Notre Dame and was named All-American. His roommate, George Gipp, became known as the "Gipper." Dutch's brothers, Alfred and Joseph, also played football at Notre Dame. Dutch went on to coach the Washington Redskins and host Dutch Bergman's Scoreboard. "When Dutch was about sixteen years old, he was very interested in the circus, especially animal training. Clyde Beatty, the famous wild animal trainer, began training Dutch with his lions at the winter quarters. Then Dutch's parents found out, and that was the end of a budding circus career," reported Susie Monahan, Dutch's daughter.
Courtesy of the Miami County Historical Society.

CHAPTER 9

Sports

Some of Miami County's first sports involved shooting matches, husking bees, pitching horseshoes, wrestling, and footraces. There were also quilting and sheep-shearing contests. Harness racing, which helped the Converse Fair grow, was popular, and children in the 1800s played town ball, the early form of today's baseball.

Winners of shooting matches might have earned themselves a turkey or a quarter of deer or beef. For a corn husking contest, the participants divided into two teams, each with about the same amount of corn. The captain who "won the toss" chose a pile for his team, and the winning team husked its pile first. Men and women both participated, and "the fellow who found a red ear of corn was entitled to the privilege of kissing the lassie next to him." And the Erie Township Fox Drive Association, formed in 1900, produced annual fox chases that became "the sport of northern Indiana."

Thoroughbred jockey James "Tod" Sloan, born in Bunker Hill in 1874, joined his brothers who were breaking horses in Chicago. Because of his short legs, Sloan devised what became known as the "Sloan" method of using short stirrups and crouching forward and low over the horse's neck. He achieved racing success in America and Europe, even racing for England's Prince of Wales. George M. Cohan loosely based his musical, Little Johnny Jones, *on Sloan's climb to fame. The musical opened successfully in 1904, but beginning in 1901, Sloan's "descent from international fame was even faster than his climb." He died penniless in Los Angeles in 1933 before Hollywood produced* Little Johnny Jones, *the film based on his life. In 1955, Sloan was elected to the National Museum's Racing Hall of Fame and in 1956, was installed in the Jockey's Hall of Fame. Courtesy of the Miami County Historical Society.*

In 1857 a convention of baseball clubs established the length of a baseball game as nine innings instead of twenty-one runs. After club owners formed the National League of Professional Base Ball Clubs in 1876, the game's popularity apparently grew. The *Peru Republican* reported the building of a new ball park in 1887, and subsequent newspaper accounts note that several baseball teams from surrounding counties traveled to Miami County to play local teams.

Baseball may be about the only sport not offered by the Young Men's Christian Association, or YMCA. The Wabash Railroad Company contributed a substantial sum of money, as did many individuals, for the first YMCA building at Eighth Street and Broadway in 1903. It had a reading room, billiard room, bowling alley, tub and shower baths, sixteen beds, and a "library of about 3,000 volumes." Today's YMCA stands at Sixth and Wabash Streets and offers sports and activities to children and adults in wrestling, swimming, basketball, soccer, volleyball, racquetball, karate, and more.

Miami County's first Fourth of July golf competition took place in 1915. The Miami County Ladies' Golf Association formed in the early 1950s with Betty Groat as its first president. Baseball and softball games have remained popular as does fishing and hunting. Golf courses, tennis courts, and bowling alleys offer participation in those sports. Schools offer football, track, swimming, wrestling, golf, basketball, and more. There's even a track at Bunker Hill for drag strip racing. And, like in older days, one can still find horse pulls and harness racing.

Miami County has had a myriad of sports and other activities going on throughout its history, but possibly some of its most distinctive activities have involved its circuses, then and now.

These students made up Peru High School's girls' basketball team in 1898, seven years after the game was developed. Courtesy of the Miami County Historical Society.

These were members of the Young Men's Christian Association 1909 basketball team. James Naismith, physical education instructor at the International YMCA training school in Massachusetts, developed the game in 1891. The YMCA and Amateur Athletic Union later established game rules based on Naismuth's thirteen axioms. Today the Miami County YMCA offers a variety of sports and sponsors one of only two YMCA circus skills programs in the United States. The other is in Baraboo, Wisconsin. Courtesy of the Miami County Historical Society.

North Grove's basketball team of 1914–1915 is shown in uniform. From left to right are: Merrill Rinker, center; Carl Haskett, guard; Gilbert Puterbaugh, guard; Ned Garber, forward; Clifford Miller, forward; and Ellis Bragg, substitute. The man in back was identified as Troyer, teacher, coach and referee. Courtesy of the Miami County Historical Society.

This unidentified man displayed his awards and photograph from the Peru Gun Club. Courtesy of the Miami County Historical Society.

Benjamin and Jessie Hight posed in their Redmon's Cubs baseball uniforms in 1929. Courtesy of the Miami County Historical Society.

Harness racing, shown here at the Converse Fair in 1938, is a major attraction there today just as it was over a century ago. The Xenia Union Agricultural Society leased land for exhibitors for the first fair in 1871. The buildings and track were built later. In the early 1900s, twenty-four passenger trains passed through Converse a day and unloaded thousands of visitors to the fair. In 1912 the fair hosted one of its first motorcycle races, and the Converse Eagle Beaks, a semi-pro baseball team, played at the fairgrounds around 1913. Courtesy of the Miami County Historical Society.

Bunker Hill's basketball team of 1940–1941 lost only two out of twenty-two games that season. Pictured left to right, back row, are: John Mills, Millburn Smith, Joe Garbert, Coach J. P. Sumpter, Bob Sonafrank, Dean Smith, and Rex Oldfather. Left to right, front row, are: Bob Foust, Mark Stazzo, Charlie Garber, Weldon Foust, and Dale Starkey. The boy is Herman Kinzie. Courtesy of the Miami County Historical Society.

Bunker Hill Naval Air Station personnel enjoyed a variety of sports, including boxing. Swimming, softball, tennis, and badminton comprised some other sport activities. Teams included the Blockbusters, football; Flying Patriots, basketball; and Bunker Hill Bluejackets, baseball. Courtesy of the Miami County Historical Society.

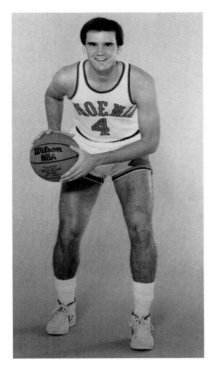

Kyle Macy, who was coached by his father and graduated from Peru High School in 1975, was named Mr. Basketball and All-American. He went on to play professional basketball for Arizona's Phoenix Suns. Courtesy of Bob and Evelyn Macy.

Area high schools have more than the standard football, basketball, and baseball teams. They have volleyball, track, and other teams. Maconaquah High School also supports swim and golf teams. This was Maconaquah High School's golf team which placed third in the 1994 state championship. From left to right are: Coach Charles Hubler, Ryan Bontrager, Matt Drinkhahn, Parker Black, Matt Plothow, and Joe Miller. Courtesy of Dale and Chris Bontrager.

This livery stable, probably located at Second and Miami Streets, belonged to Ben Wallace who established Peru's circus winter quarters. In 1881 the Peru Republican *reported the stable to be the largest in Indiana. Courtesy of Jerry Wise.*

CHAPTER 10

Circuses

Before Ben Wallace bought his first circus animals and established his first circus winter quarters in the 1880s, circuses traveled to Miami County, and county newspapers contained ads spreading the wonder, glitter, and color of such circuses before newspaper readers.

As early as May, 1872, the *Peru Republican* advertised Adam Forepaugh's Celebrated Zoological and Equestrian Aggregation. The name may have been long, but so was its list of attractions. The attractions included two miles of cages, 595 men and animals, a herd each of camels and elephants, one thousand magnificent birds, and ten thousand great curiosities under four tents. Chang-Eng, the two-headed baby, was billed as the star attraction. And the price to see all of it was fifty cents for adults and twenty-five cents for children under ten.

Two months later the same newspaper carried an advertisement advising "look out for the Boss—the Great Mastodon of the World." C. W.

Noyes Great Crescent City Circus and Caravan was bringing "the Boss" along with "50 performing horses" and a pavilion "lighted with gas instead of oil." The circus also brought along Dr. Thayer, "the largest clown in America," who performed with his mules. Following in July, the Sells Brothers Mammoth Quadruple Alliance was billed as museum, menagerie, caravan, and circus with "a solid mile of gorgeous splendor and a continent of canvas." And before July ended, another *Republican* ad listed the Great Eastern Museum, Menagerie, Aviary, Circus and Balloon Show as "the only six-tent show requiring 70 railroad cars to transport it." Accompanying the show were "407 men and horses" and "105 animals," which included wolves, camels, Mexican and silver lions, a grizzly bear, a long-legged boar of Arkansas, and laughing hyenas.

Wallace began collecting circus animals, wagons, and equipment before he bought his first winter quarters in 1881 with profits from his livery barn. The animals resided at the quarters located east of Peru along what is now Indiana 124 on a farm owned by Jim and Barb Poor, and Sullivan and Eagle wagon works overhauled fifty wagons and cages for Wallace. His mother lived in a house on the property and helped with canning and other activities. His wife and her sister sewed the performers' wardrobe. In 1884, a show bill announced "Wallace and Co.'s Great World's Menagerie and International Circus at Peru." It gave its first performance, and Peru's brass band led the street procession.

Then in 1891, Wallace bought the 220-acre farm of Gabriel Godfroy located west of the winter quarters. He also purchased five acres in the north end of Peru to be used as a railroad for his rail cars. Over the next several years he bought and sold various circuses while building up the winter quarters until the

This rare brick barn stands on the site of Ben Wallace's first circus winter quarters along what is now Indiana 124 east of Peru. Jim and Barb Poor, who own the farm, opened Poor Farm Candies in the brick farmhouse in 1986. Wallace bought the farm in 1881. Local folklore says if one closely examines the barn's old timbers, one might discover the claw marks of lions and tigers caged there over a century ago. Wallace's mother lived in a house on the property and helped with canning and other activities. His wife and sister sewed the circus's wardrobe. Courtesy of the Miami County Historical Society.

1913 flood wiped his circus out financially. Though forced to sell the Hagenbeck-Wallace title and equipment that year, he kept the winter quarters until his death in 1921. His heirs then sold six hundred acres and buildings of the quarters plus the railroad track to the American Circus Corporation. Between 1921 and 1931, various circuses came and went. Among them were Hagenbeck-Wallace, John Robinson, Howes Great London Shows, and Sells-Floto.

The ACC, under management of Jerry Mugivan, Bert Bowers, and Edward Ballard, refurbished the winter quarters. It had its own water system drawn from the Mississinewa, its own fire protection, and electricity purchased from the local light plant. At one time there existed four ring barns, a paint shop, a dormitory with bath tubs for circus workers, a steel arena, two dining halls, a cage house, and other buildings. A pastor of the First Presbyterian Church, accompanied by "a miniature organ and an abridged choir," even offered services in the elephant barn on Sundays where between one hundred fifty and two hundred circus performers and workers gathered. And not only could elephants, horses, and big cats be found, but bears, kangaroos, deer, goats, and dogs, too. The 1920s brought in big money for the circuses. By 1929 the year John Ringling bought all ACC's holdings, Peru appeared on maps as the circus city. However, the 1930s were the Depression years, and one by one the circuses folded. By 1941 the decision to close the quarters and sell them was made. Wagons that weren't removed by Ringling to its winter quarters in Sarasota, Florida, or sold were burned. Emil Schram of the New York Stock Exchange

Gabriel Godfroy posed at home with his son, George Durand Godfroy, circa 1903. Godfroy, who wore a blanket that belonged to the famous Frances Slocum, sold to Ben Wallace in 1891 his 220-acre farm which belonged to his father, Chief Francis Godfroy. Godfroy received the land from the U.S. government in 1826. Courtesy of the Miami County Historical Society.

The elephant Charlie walked beside his trainer, Henry Hoffman, when this photograph was taken before 1899. In 1901 Charlie beat Hoffman to death against a log platform anchored at the river's edge right in front of the winter quarters. Charlie was later destroyed. Courtesy of the Miami County Historical Society.

then bought the winter quarters, and later sold it to Peru native Lyman Bond, an Indianapolis stockbroker.

Meanwhile the Circus City Festival formed, and two years later an amateur circus, often trained by former circus greats that had retired to Peru, began performing. The former winter quarters continued to serve as a farm. Then in 1981 Sarasota's Circus Hall of Fame collection came up for sale. Indiana residents, business groups, and the state government gave $450,000 for the collection and moved it to Peru. In 1988 the former winter quarters became a National Historic Landmark, and Bond's goal was to see it preserved and restored. In 1989 he offered it to the International Circus Hall of Fame. In 1991 the centennial anniversary of the circus winter quarters was celebrated with circus performances on the grounds. Two years later a museum opened in one of the barns, and today people can again visit the site where elephants once watered and the big cats roared.

The Wabash Valley Trust Company opened in 1904 on the southwest corner of Broadway and Main Street with Ben Wallace as president. He needed a financial institution that would handle all of his circus's money. The building eventually housed circus offices and a circus wardrobe. Courtesy of Otis Marks.

Wallace's first circus set up to perform on Armstrong Avenue in South Peru, then later about where Mace Food Store stands today. "In the wee hours of the morning we could hear the wagons, horses, and elephants moving in since we now lived across the street from the show grounds. We could watch from our beds the unloading and after the performances, the loading of the circus wagons . . . The circus liked to water the elephants from the hose in front of our house. At one time, there were eighty elephants lined up," recalled Dorothy Cunningham in 1961. Courtesy of the Miami County Historical Society.

A mother elephant was photographed at winter quarters with her reflection cast in a puddle. Courtesy of the Miami County Historical Society.

Men with teams of mules cultivated corn on one of Ben Wallace's farms. At one time twenty-seven hundred acres were farmed. *Courtesy of Jerry Wise.*

Sullivan and Eagle crafted this circus wagon at their shop at 25 West Canal Street in Peru. "An old truck would slowly pull two or three wagons out to the winter quarters after they had been painted. So we'd jump onto the last wagon and sneak out to the winter quarters that way . . . It was really something out there. We'd sneak around and look at the elephants and horses, but not at the tigers or lions if they were roaring. They were scary," re-called Bill Redmon *in* Playing With Lions and Other Circus Tales. *Courtesy of the Miami County Historical Society.*

The 1913 flood, which wiped out Wallace's circus financially, killed elephants and other circus animals at the winter quarters. "By Tuesday morning the elephants were standing in three feet of water, which continued to rise at the rate of seven inches an hour . . . They stood quietly while the men swam under water and removed the heavy chains holding the elephants to the floor . . . Trainer Worden would have drowned if it were not for "Nellie" who lifted him off the floor . . . and carried him to the house." Nellie left, then returned with other elephants which beat down doors and broke windows trying to get in the house. "Then the trainer was forced upstairs by the rising water. He watched the elephants pace around the house, but noticed their number decreasing . . . having sunk beneath the waves and drowned," from Our Circus Heritage by Debbie Rose Fishback. Courtesy of the Miami County Historical Society.

This aerial photograph taken of the circus winter quarters, possibly in the 1920s, shows the many barns and other buildings that housed animals, training rings, sleeping quarters, wagon shop, and other areas. Many of the buildings have since burned or been torn down. Courtesy of the Miami County Historical Society.

These clowns performed for the Hagenbeck-Wallace Circus, circa 1931. Courtesy of the Miami County Historical Society.

This photograph of cowboy movie star Tom Mix, center in white cowboy hat, was taken with the Peru Chamber of Commerce and an eighth-grade class in 1934. Mix, who was eventually inducted into the International Circus Hall of Fame, left the movie screen for the Sells-Floto Circus ring from 1929 to 1932. The circus wintered at Peru. Mix wore his cowboy attire on the streets and lived in a special railroad parlor car near Washington Avenue. "I probably visited him fifteen times over on Washington, but the rules were we couldn't cross the street. Mix always sat on his cement porch with his Cord car out front. And he would always wave," recalled Bill Redmon in Tom Mix and the Circus. Courtesy of the Miami County Historical Society.

In 1940 famous wild animal trainer Terrell Jacobs, who had performed with Ringling-Barnum shows, bought land along U.S. 31 about seven miles south of Peru. He brought his animals and presented a rodeo circus in 1941. In 1942 the Circus Model Builders of America met there. Jacobs wintered at the farm and toured with other circuses until 1944 when the Terrell Jacobs Wild Animal Circus opened in Peru with Tom Mix's brother, Art. Jacobs later had to sell the farm when his wife divorced him. Paul and Dorothy Kelly, who still own the farm, bought the place about 1955. Courtesy of the Miami County Historical Society.

Wild animal trainer Terrell Jacobs posed with nine lions. He owned the circus farm not far from DeLoris Welden's home. "One time Terrell let me in a cage with an old tiger. It probably didn't have any teeth, but he handed me a big old chair I could hardly hold and he gave me a whip, and I just thought I was the biggest thing. Of course, I was a young teenager then . . . The tiger didn't really do anything but get up on its perch," recalled DeLoris Welden. Courtesy of the Miami County Historical Society.

This photograph depicts the remains of circus wagons that were burned in 1940 after the decision was made to sell the winter quarters. Some band wagons and tableaux were saved, and some wagons were shipped to Sarasota, Florida. All too many ended their usefulness in flames and were sold for scrap iron despite residents who pleaded to buy them. In 1944 the last five circus wagons that had been stored in Peru were shipped out. *Courtesy of the Miami County Historical Society.*

Dorothy Kelly originally worked as a buyer for a Chicago department store and married Paul Kelly. Though born into a circus family, Paul worked as a truck driver and a manager of an auto shop before joining the circus. Dorothy later trained circus animals and performed with elephants. Once she performed with a cut on her foot and two broken toes after an elephant stepped on them. *Courtesy of the Miami County Historical Society.*

Peru's first amateur circus group performed under a tent on the lot behind the tennis courts at Third and Benton Streets in 1960. Bunker Hill Air Force Base, later named Grissom, put on a sideshow involving forty people in conjunction with the circus. Courtesy of Ollie Miller.

The Peru Lumber Company at Broadway and Seventh Street became the site of today's Circus City Center. Peru's amateur circus performed there in 1968. Bleachers had been installed, but there was no roof. Today the building contains a circus museum, gift shop, ticket office, wardrobe, three rings, and a back lot. Performances are given every year in July with a circus parade highlighting the final Saturday of performances. Courtesy of Otis Marks.

Kate Cole, who married Samuel F. Porter, reportedly changed their son's name to a four-letter one—Cole—because she was told a four-letter name would be lucky. By age six Cole Porter was practicing music two hours a day. At age ten he wrote words and music for a song dedicated to his mother. At around age fourteen he was standby pianist at Peru's movie houses and writing and directing plays for his school. As an adult, he broke into Broadway with music for Two Big Eyes. *Among his other musical stage production credits was* Kiss Me, Kate, *which was made into a motion picture. Porter's favorite candy, which he ordered from wherever he was in the world until he died, was So-Good fudge made by Arnold's Candies of Peru. Courtesy of the Miami County Historical Society.*

CHAPTER II

Cole Porter and the Arts

The arts aren't limited to a painting, a song, a sculpture, a dance, or a book. Art includes plays, movies, and crafts, too. Artists evolve from all kinds of people and sometimes art just touches people's lives for a time in one way or another.

People thought of the arts early. The Peru Lecture Association, organized in 1878, furnished "musical and literary entertainments." The Peru Chautauqua Literary and Scientific Circle was established in 1886 as was the Peru Reading Club. Shortly thereafter, the Peru Literary Club formed, and the Monday Night Literary Club formed in 1892 to study U.S. history. And through the years, Miami County had its own authors. Mrs. D. M. Jordan wrote *Rosemary Leaves*, which was published in 1873 and dedicated "affectionately" to her mother and sisters. Mary Edna White, born in 1883, first wrote a one-act

play, *Official Bondage*. Her later works included *Sacrifice, Lies*, and *Mecurial Youth*, but she was best known for *The Life of Paul*.

Al W. Martin got his start in show business selling tickets when he traveled with Ben Wallace's circuses in spring and summer. During the winter seasons, Martin earned "a barrel of money" through his show, *Uncle Tom's Cabin* which played at Chicago, Brooklyn, and other places. However, Miami County has produced performers, too. Movie stars Leota, Dorothy, and Priscilla Mullican were born in Macy after 1900 to Dr. Leonard and Cora Hicks Mullican. They and another sister, Rosemary, who was born in Indianolo, Iowa, later took the stage name of Lane.

Dorothy adopted the name "Lola" and composed several songs. Leota trained her voice for musical comedy and light opera and played the leading role in Victor Herbert's *Babes in Toyland* in 1930. They appeared in a sister act together at New York and less than two months later received a two-month engagement to sing in London. Rosemary, who also sang, was an accomplished pianist at age thirteen. In 1930 she and Priscilla starred in a singing and dancing act with Stanley Smith in a stage show in Des Moines, Iowa. Priscilla co-starred with Cary Grant in Frank Capra's *Arsenic and Old Lace* which played at Peru's Roxy Theater in 1944. Eventually all four sisters starred in motion pictures.

Early on, residents also appreciated drama and art. In 1916, to help celebrate Indiana's centennial as a state, the better part of a hundred people or more, Native American and white, put on *Maconaquah*, a pageant rather fancifully portraying the life of Frances Slocum, a white woman the Miamis called Maconaquah. The Peru Drama Club celebrated its fiftieth, and last, year at the end of the 1961–1962 season. In 1964 the Ole Olsen Memorial Theater was officially formed with *Come Blow Your Horn* as its first play and *Music Man* as its first musical. And the Peru Art Club was founded in 1900 with its purpose being the "study, appreciation, and encouragement of art."

Facing page: John "Ole" Olsen was born in Peru in 1891. He and Chic Johnson teamed up for a vaudeville act beginning in 1914. Their first full-scale musical, Hellzapoppin, *played to "1,040 roaring (sold out) houses" in New York before going on the road. Between 1930 and 1945, the pair played in eleven movies, among them* Hellzapoppin *and* Ghost Catchers. *Before their career ended they played throughout the United States and in Canada, Australia, and Europe, appearing before presidents and royalty, but Ole never forgot his hometown for he visited it often. "May you live as long as you want to and laugh as long as you live," was the philosophy of Ole Olsen and Chic Johnson. Courtesy of the Miami County Historical Society.*

Actress Joan Crawford appeared with Don Donaldson, center, and Bill Donaldson from Denver in this 1934 photograph. Before then the brothers "rode their thumbs to California" to attend college, but fell on hard times. One brother, who worked in a beauty parlor where Crawford had her hair done, found a dollar on the floor one day, a dollar he sorely needed, but returned. Crawford heard about the good deed and became the boys' mentor, paying their college bills. Omer Holman, **Peru Republican** *publisher, dedicated an edition of the newspaper to Crawford on her twenty-sixth birthday, March 23, 1934. Nearly eight hundred birthday greetings were sent to Crawford from the Denver area. As for the brothers, one became a barber in Van Nuys, California. The other opened a ceramic shop in Los Angeles. Courtesy of the Miami County Historical Society*

And one didn't have to possess a well-known name or reputation to gain appreciation for one's art. Emma Monce got a letter of congratulations on her ninety-third birthday in 1961 from J. Edward Roush, Democratic representative from her Fifth District, and a request from him for one of her paintings. She sent him one, and he hung it on his office wall in Washington. Monce, who lived at Mexico's Old Folks Home, began painting when she was seventy-five years old and produced over one hundred thirty paintings, most of them landscapes. She sat by a window with a canvas in her lap and painted scenes mostly drawn from postcards and pictures in magazines. Those paintings she didn't give away, she sold for twenty-five dollars a piece.

One woman, whose name Miami County may never know, earned appreciation from the art world for a quilt she sewed over a century ago. Considered to be a "one-of-a-kind," the quilt was advertised for sale in New York City and valued at twenty thousand dollars around 1984. Thomas K. Woodard of American Antiques and Quilts, who owned the quilt, described the quilt as navy on white, appliqued by an invalid Peru resident, and depicting her view of the Erie Railroad. The letters "E" and "R" appear on the quilt along with the year 1888. No one seems to know who the woman was that sewed the quilt, but that doesn't lessen its value. "Anything figural is very rare and very desirable, like a folk art painting," Woodard was quoted as saying.

Reading, writing, producing plays, acting, and sewing, however, weren't the only ways in which women distinguished themselves. One often reads about the political, civic, and related accomplishments of a county's men, but sometimes very little about the similar deeds of its women.

Ross F. Lockridge, right, a Peru educator and later an Indiana University professor of history, wrote several books on Indiana history. His son, Ross Lockridge Jr., left, wrote the prize-winning novel, Raintree County, in 1948 which became a movie starring Elizabeth Taylor. His cousin, center, Mary Jane Ward, wrote The Snake Pit, an exposé of conditions in a state-run mental institutions of the 1940s. Courtesy of the Miami County Historical Society.

G. David Thompson, who graduated from Peru High School in 1913, became a prominent Pittsburg, Pennsylvania, industrialist and philanthropist who didn't forget his old school. In 1945 he presented Peru High School with an "outstanding" art collection in honor of his favorite teacher, John Whittenberger. Courtesy of the Miami County Historical Society.

Artist Art Johns started by painting signs and scenery for the Hagenbeck-Wallace and Cole Brothers circuses. Later he was placed in charge of the paint shop at Bunker Hill Naval Air Base. Courtesy of the Miami County Historical Society.

Leon Allen, a Bunker Hill undertaker, drove his hearse and horses at Miami County's Rankin Cemetery as part of a funeral procession scene for the movie Fanny Crosby. *The movie, filmed in 1983, depicted the life of Crosby who wrote over nine thousand religious and secular songs. Producer-director Ken Anderson saw a photograph of Allen's hearse and contacted him. Allen suggested Rankin Cemetery for the scene because the original funeral took place during the mid-1800s. Thus the scene could have no power lines or modern grave markers. The scene had to be re-shot once when a car back-fired and a jet flew overhead. Courtesy of Leon Allen.*

Movie star Audie Murphy and a starlet visited Peru in 1959 for the movie premier of The Big Circus. *Nearly thirty years earlier, Admiral Richard Byrd visited Peru to promote the movie about his South Pole expedition. In 1971, NBC aired "Circus Town USA" which showcased Peru's amateur circus. It later placed first in the American Film Festival as best children's film. Courtesy of the Miami County Historical Society.*

Tim Noble, singer, director, writer, and actor, graduated as salutatorian from Peru High School in 1963. In 1972 he appeared in the Broadway show The Selling of the President *and has appeared on the Ed Sullivan and Mike Douglas television shows. His operatic career began in 1981 with the San Francisco Opera. Since then he has performed in most major opera houses in North America and Europe and has directed an opera. He has also published several choral works. Courtesy of Tim Noble.*

THE MAYFLOWER.

DEVOTED TO THE INTERESTS OF WOMAN.

"TEMPERANCE, PURITY, AND HAPPY HOMES."

| Volume 1. | PERU, INDIANA, MARCH 1, 1861. | Number 5. |

THE MAYFLOWER,

A SEMI-MONTHLY QUARTO,

Devoted to Literature and the Elevation of
WOMAN.

PUBLISHED AT PERU, IND., BY

MISS LIZZIE BUNNELL,

EDITOR AND PROPRIETOR.

MARY F. THOMAS, M. D.,

OF RICHMOND, IND., ASSOCIATE EDITOR.

TERMS—Fifty Cents a Year, in advance, or Eleven copies for Five Dollars.

☞Office at Home Cottage, Peru.

☞Local subscriptions may be left at the Republican Office, in Peru, where specien copies may always be seen.

☞All coummnications and remittances should be addressed to Miss Lizzie Bunnell, Peru, Miami Co., Indiana.

"It is More Blessed."

BY ROSE TERRY.

Give! as the morning that flows out of heaven;
Give! as the waves when their channel is riven;
Give! as the free air and sunshine are given;
    Lavishly, utterly, carelessly give.
Not the waste drops of thy cup overflowing,
Not the faint sparks of thy hearth ever glowing,
Not a pale bud from the June roses blowing;
    Give, as He gave thee, who gave thee to live.

Pour out thy love, like the rush of a river
Wasting its waters, forever and ever,
Through the burnt sands that reward not the giver;
    Silent or songful, thou nearest the sea.
Scatter thy life as the summer showers pouring!
What if no bird through the pearl-rain is soaring?
What if no blossom looks upward adoring?
    Look to the life that was lavished for thee.

Give! though thy heart may be wasted and weary,
Laid on an altar all ashen and dreary;
Though from its pulses a sad miserere
    Beats to thy soul the sad presage of fate;
Bind it with cords of unshrinking devotion,
Smile at the song of its restless emotion,
'Tis the stern hymn of eternity's ocean,
    Hear! and in silence thy future await.

So the wild wind strews its perfumed caresses,
Evil and thankless the desert it blesses,
Bitter the wave that its soft pinion presses,
    Never it ceaseth to whisper and sing.
What if the hard heart give thorns for thy roses?
What if on rocks thy tired bosom reposes?
Sweetest is music with minor-keyed closes,
    Fairest the vines that on ruin will cling.

Almost the day of thy giving is over;
Ere from the grass dies the bee haunted clover,
Thou wilt have vanished from friend and from lover,
    Naught shall thy longing avail in the grave.
Give, as the heart gives, whose fetters are breaking,

Physical and Intellectual Development of Woman.

BY REV. G. S. WEAVER.

Concluded.

Though the mass of women in all countries have been intellectually undeveloped, we have instances enough to show that the woman-mind is as powerful, close sighted and active as man's. Women have ruled the mightiest nations, mastered the abstruse sciences, led vigorous armies to victory, written powerful books, made vigorous achievements in eloquence, commanded vessels, conducted complicated commercial relations, edited influential journals and papers, sat in chairs of learning, and done everything necessary to show that the female mind is not wanting in power. Yet if the female mind were weaker, it is not an argument against its education. Mind should be educated, whether little or much, weak or strong. And woman's natural position is such, that all the mind she has should be developed and richly cultivated.

We talk much about female education; we have female schools and colleges; and one might think, to read of them, that we educated the female mind. But it is a sad mistake. The greater part of our female seminaries and colleges are mere shams. They do not develop mind; they do not train its muscles to hard work; they do not discipline its nerves to close application and vigorous research; they do not harden its hands to the toil of thinking, nor strengthen its arms to battle with the intricacies of science nor the problems of metaphysics. They are mere gilding shops, white-washing establishments, paint factories, where girls are polished to order with the etiquette of boarding school finish.

We send our girls to these schools to be educated; but educated for what? Why, nothing in particular; but to be educated because it is fashionable; to go home and sit in the parlor "educated ladies;" to talk about novels and poetry with the gentlemen that come in; to go into extacies over some boy's *last!* to set up for a professional husband. It is to go *over*, not *through* some of the sciences, but do it because it is fashionable; recite and write, and go through all the forms of school training, just because it sounds well and will give a lady social position, not literary standing or scientific character, intellectual influence, or dignity of thought and life; and go through it all, and graduate with diploma in hand at fourteen or sixteen years of age.

Here again women are cheated with a bauble. Little girls are told that they are educated at this tender age, and to prove it are referred to their diplomas,

at such an institution. Only think of it—a finished education at sixteen! Why, the majority of our young men cannot get ready for college till they are twenty or twenty-five. There they spend four years in hard study and the most vigorous mental discipline, delving in the deep mines of science, and untombing the rich archives of history and human thought; then study three years the masters of their professions. And even then they are but boys in thought and action, and must meet the hard discipline of active life, before we award to them intellectual manhood. We compare these educated girls with these educated young men, and wonder at the weakness of the female mind! The girls went to school because it was fashionable; the boys at the call of an honorable ambition. The girls studied to appear well in society; the boys to tread life's highway with honor and win laurels from the hand of the world in the duties of useful professions. The girls were stimulated by nothing that was great and noble in action; the boys were fired by all that can stir up human ambition. True, the innate glory of cultivated minds was before them both, but that alone in our present sensuous life, has seldom been found a sufficient stimulus to vigorous intellectual discipline.—I should be glad to see a class of our strongest young women go through Dartmouth, Yale and Cambridge colleges with the same preparation and stimulants that our young men possess. If I mistake not, they would graduate with honors, and be heard from in the high field of intellectual life.

But as this cannot be at present, our young women must make the best of the opportunities they have. What education they do get should be thorough, practical and from proper motives. They must fill woman's place, and they ought to prepare for it as thoroughly as possible. They have an intellectual life to live and intellectual duties to perform. How poorly they will live that life and perform those duties without a preparation. Many young women cannot attend school and enjoy the common routine of mental discipline; but they may read and study at home; they may cultivate their minds by the fireside, in the lecture room, in the church, and in the intellectual circle.—The midnight hour may impart strength to their minds, and the morning dawn may find them storing them with useful knowledge. The world is full of good books, and from them they may glean invaluable treasures. Every young woman spends time enough in idle gossip and foolish flirtation to educate herself well. Schools are not necessary—they are only helps to education. Many great minds have been educated without them. To educate is to learn to think. The way to learn to think is to practice thinking—

Women of Distinction

They raised families and food, supported their husbands' achievements, helped homestead, and founded South Peru. They published a newspaper, served as nurses during times of war and serviced airplanes, traveled around the world, and obtained the right for women to vote. They were women, rich and poor, famous and unknown, but they were all women of distinction. One usually reads much about what men did in building and contributing to a county, but sometimes little is recorded about the contributions of its women.

Ellen Walker Shirk, who proposed the formation of the Peru Associated Charities in 1891, became its first woman president a few years later. During the 1913 flood, the Associated Charities served sandwiches at the courthouse. But women didn't just run charities or own hat shops. Mrs. William Mercer, Mrs. Avery Tudor, and Mrs. Walter Emswiler organized Mercer-Kier Oil Company in the 1890s, which was among the most successful of the dozens of oil companies formed. In 1902 Martha

This was how Frances Slocum, shown in the upper left hand corner, looked late in life. Her family searched for her for years after she was captured as a child in Pennsylvania by Delaware Indians. She was discovered living amongst the Miami Indians near Peru in 1835 by George Ewing, a trader with the Miamis. Slocum died in 1847, but the monument wasn't erected until 1900. Her descendants, Mabel and Victoria Bundy, appear in the picture as do William and Gabriel Godfroy, sons of the last Miami war chief. Gabriel, right, married a granddaughter of Slocum. Remaining members of Slocum's white family tried to get her to return to Pennsylvania, but she refused, saying the Miamis respected her and treated her well. She wanted to be buried beside her husband, a Miami chief, and their two sons. Courtesy of the Miami County Historical Society.

G. Shirk served as Peru Public Library's first librarian. Gertrude H. Thiebaud became her assistant.

During World War I, Harriett Carfree received a citation for work with the British Red Cross. She arrived in France in 1915 and at her own request, was detailed to help care for wounded American soldiers. At about the same time Frannie Effington married Erwin Raymond and moved to San Francisco where she went to work for the Gregg Publishing Company. There she helped develop the speed writing called shorthand, and by 1912, she had become publisher. In 1917 she received a medal of honor for her achievement at the San Francisco Exposition in enhancing American education.

Mary Trent, who started work at Redmon's basket factory in 1922, received recognition in a 1959 newspaper photograph for driving "tacks into the basket with incredible speed and accuracy. When asked if she ever missed and hit her fingers, she replied, "Oh yes, many times, but I just don't pay any attention to it." In later years Linda Schanlaub made some news in a business usually dominated by men. Schanlaub, who has never lived on a farm, went from working behind the desk of a large agricultural firm around 1990 to owning and running Macy Elevator. Though the profession is one usually dominated by men, Schanlaub enjoys it and her success. "The business is growing steadily. There's only a few small elevators left in the county . . . But I believe there's still customers out there who need a small town elevator," said Linda Schanlaub, owner and manager of Macy Elevator.

Thanks to Betty Stone, needy Miami County children in first through twelfth grades receive dental care. In 1958 Stone began managing the "dental clinic," an agency first backed by Delta Theta Tau sorority then Beta Sigma Phi sorority, and financially supported by United Way. The dental clinic pays for dental work for needy children in Miami County from first through twelfth grades. Stone provides transportation to dental appointments, toothbrushes, and related items out of her own pocket.

In the 1960s, she and her late husband, Russell, convinced Peru officials to move girls' softball games from Davis Park to West City Park. "We crawled on our hands and knees, dragging a bucket around, picking up rocks and marking off the diamond," recalled Betty Stone about working on the girls first softball diamond at West City Park.

Other women have spent years gathering information vital to the heritage of the Miami Indians. Like her mother, Anna Mongosa Marks, Carmen Ryan served on the Miami Indian tribal council, and became tribal genealogist and historian. She traveled widely, accompanied by Lora Siders, doing most of the research work when treaty payments were made in 1969 and 1973. "She got several people on tribal rolls who weren't on them because several people had denied their Indian heritage. They might have lost their jobs because of it, but she got them on the rolls without getting them into trouble. When Carmen came to the place she couldn't do this any more, she insisted I take over, and I did. I've just tried to keep us together" (Interview with Lora Siders, Miami Indian genealogist and tribal historian, 1995).

Katy Brown, born on a Tennessee plantation, was adopted into the family as a playmate for the children. At age fifteen she was sold to another planter for one hundred fifty dollars. She was sold several times through the years until she escaped from one owner to care for a member of the Cole family she had grown up with. After he died, Brown went with Union soldiers to Nashville, Tennessee, and eventually came to Peru. It was "largely through her push and energy that the colored church and parsonage on East Third Street were built." Courtesy of the Miami County Historical Society.

Emma Davidson was elected state librarian in 1895. Mrs. Wesley Haynes of Miami County was the first woman to hold the position of state librarian. A Peru school teacher, Eileen Ahern, also took the position. Courtesy of the Miami County Historical Society.

This diploma records Mary Sharp as Miami County's first graduate nurse. She was born in 1874 and died in 1942. Courtesy of the Miami County Historical Society.

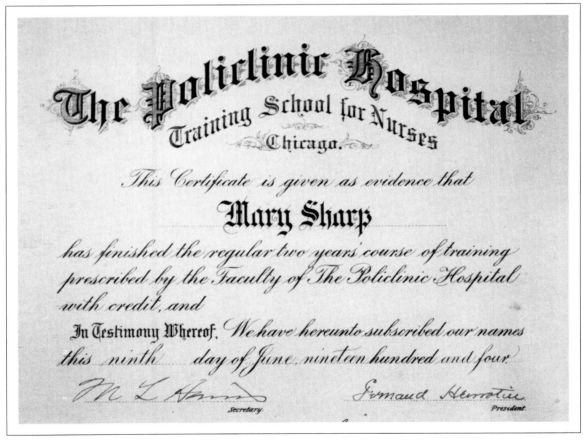

The Policlinic Hospital
Training School for Nurses
Chicago.

This Certificate is given as evidence that

Mary Sharp

has finished the regular two years' course of training prescribed by the Faculty of The Policlinic Hospital with credit, and

In Testimony Whereof, We have hereunto subscribed our names this ninth day of June nineteen hundred and four

Secretary.

President.

Edith Lees and Louise Chum worked as bakers at the Mexico orphanage. Levi Miller founded the Home for Old Folks and Orphans in 1889 with help from the Middle Indiana District of the Church of the Brethren. The orphanage closed in 1943, but the home for the adults re-mained open until 1968 when it was moved to North Manchester in adjoining Wabash County and became Timbercrest. Courtesy of the Miami County Historical Society.

This was the women's German Aide Society during World War I. Courtesy of the Miami County Historical Society.

Marie Edwards, who served as first vice president of the National League of Women Voters, stood to the left of President Warren Harding in Washington, D.C. sometime during his term from 1921 to 1923. Edwards was part of the League delegation meeting with the president. The other women were League officers from other states. Edwards, a civic leader, also served as Peru School Board's first woman member. Courtesy of the Miami County Historical Society.

"We're the suffragets. We wear the trousers," was the caption of this undated photograph. None of the women were identified. Courtesy of the Miami County Historical Society.

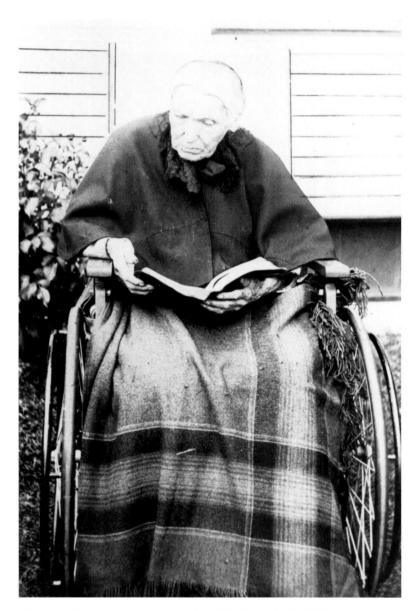

As much as Hal C. Phelps contributed to the courthouse museum, Caroline Puterbaugh contributed to the Peru Public Library museum annex. Puterbaugh, a "great lover of bird and animal life and deeply interested in civic affairs," died in the 1920s. She bequeathed twelve thousand dollars for the annex and ten thousand dollars for its upkeep. A great many items came to call the museum annex home, but when the Miami County Museum opened, the annex collection joined the courthouse collection at the new museum. Courtesy of the Miami County Historical Society.

Elizabeth Barnhisel, shown here on her 103rd birthday in 1933, was the widow of a Civil War veteran. She received a letter dated July 1863 reportedly notifying her of her husband's death in Alexandria, Louisiana, some decades after he died. She died in 1934 before her 104th birthday. "When we came to this farm it was all forest. We built our own log house, and we helped build the first church on our farm," recalled Barnhisel who homesteaded near Gilead in 1852. Courtesy of the Miami County Historical Society.

The first WAVES reported to Bunker Hill Naval Air Station in 1943 and gradually replaced sailors in key positions such as radio technicians, tower control, link trainer operators, parachute, and aviation machinist mates. Courtesy of the Miami County Historical Society.

Dorothy Crossland, who organized the local branch of the NAACP in 1946, retired as an avid worker and supporter of the NAACP in 1975 after thirty-one years. Her family moved from Charlestown, Indiana, to Peru in 1926 because of racial prejudice. "High schools in the southern counties were segregated then, and my sister and brothers had to get up before daylight, walk one and a half miles to the railroad station and ride a train seventeen miles to New Albany. Then they walked another three miles and passed two more high schools to reach the inferior facility for Negroes," recalled Dorothy Crossland about racial prejudice. Courtesy of the Miami County Historical Society.

Mary L. Guillaume taught in Peru Community Schools from 1928 to 1975 and started the first Miami County spelling bee. She also instituted the Fireman-Policeman Benefit Basketball game for the March of Dimes and served as state chairman of the elementary department of the Indiana State Teachers Association. She was the senior queen of Miami County in 1985–1986 and a member of the Miami County Historical Society, Circus City Festival, and Dukes Memorial Hospital Auxiliary. Courtesy of Charlotte Bohm and Ava Middlekauff.

Patricia Cunningham, daughter of Mr. and Mrs. Clyde Cunningham of Peru, represented Indiana in the Miss America pageant of 1949. Courtesy of the Miami County Historical Society.

Betty Rendel first became involved with politics when she served as Fifth District Vice Chairman for the Goldwater for President campaign in 1964. She was elected vice chairman of the Miami County Republican Central Committee, president of the Miami County Women's Club, and director of the Fifth District for the Indiana Federation of Republican Women. She served as president of the National Federation of Republican Women from 1980 to 1985. Under her leadership, NFRW expanded its budget and its programs, providing greater support to Republican candidates and to women in politics. In 1986 Rendel was appointed for a three-year term to the Defense Advisory Committee of Women in the Services by President Reagan. Courtesy of Betty Rendel.

Ilona Conway, daughter of Mr. and Mrs. Vernon Conway of Bunker Hill, was named Miss Indiana in 1982 after her third try for the title. She was Miss Miami County in 1977. Courtesy of Fincher Photos.

Sara Stalker has volunteered her time and money as one of Indiana's few licensed wildlife rehabilitators for over thirty years. Her love of animals developed in childhood. "My dad said I had a gift. The animals never bit me. I would pick up animals that bit other people. I truly believe God put me here at this time at this place to do this because it's needed. There are so few people who really care about wildlife," she says. Courtesy of the author.

Vesper Wilkinson Cook was a researcher for the Indiana Historical Society before being appointed Miami County Historian by the Indiana Histori-cal Bureau in 1981. She served as curator of the Miami County Museum and Puterbaugh Museum from 1961 to 1983. She was listed in Who's Who of American Women *from 1964 to 1969 and again in 1979. From 1965 to 1983 she was a biographer in* Who's Who in the Midwest. *She has written numerous booklets and articles on Miami County history. "I've been interested in history all my life. My mother was interested, too. I think history must have interested a great deal of the family because her aunt was interested in history and genealogy, too," reported Vesper Cook in 1995.*

Cole Porter as a child waved a flag from his father's drugstore booth. His father, Samuel, stands in a suit on the right. The occasion was Peru's first street fair. "The fantastic booths, which extend into the street along the whole length of Broadway, are built in every conceivable style of architecture, and are crowded with wares of all sorts," reported the Peru Republican, 1894. Courtesy of the Miami County Historical Society.

CHAPTER 13

Leisure Activities

W hen people could take time from the work of raising families and food and making a living, they enjoyed leisure activities like church socials and watched their children at school exhibit their knowledge of spelling and arithmetic. At other times people held literary and other forms of debate and they enjoyed dancing and music.

At one time nearly every community, large and small, had a band. Other kinds of musical groups existed, too, like the Peru Choral Union and the Peru Musical Association. People sang and enjoyed opera at local opera houses. They attended plays, went to the circus, fireworks, and carnivals, and lined up for circus, political, Labor Day, and homecoming parades. They went to parks for ice cream socials, games, and picnics and they joined a wide variety of groups and clubs which offered fun, fellowship, and shared experiences.

These men were members of the 1888 Zither Club. Courtesy of the Miami County Historical Society.

The Masonic fraternity was one of the first "secret" orders to establish itself in the county. Lodges developed in Peru, Xenia, Miami, Mexico, Gilead, Macy, Chili, Bunker Hill, and North Grove. The Independent Order of Odd Fellows followed the Masonic fraternity and established lodges in Peru, Miami, Chili, Converse, Bunker Hill, Mexico, Macy, Deedsville, Denver, and Amboy. The Daughters of Rebekah, composed of the wives, mothers, and sisters of the Odd Fellows, developed groups in connection with some of the lodges. The Knights of Pythias formed lodges in Miami, Bunker Hill, Converse, Denver, and Peru. The one established at Macy was short-lived.

The Grand Army of the Republic, composed of soldiers who served in the Civil War, organized five posts in Miami County in 1882. The posts located at Peru, Converse, Denver, Macy, and Bunker Hill. The Women's Relief Corps, composed of the wives and daughters of the members of the GAR, had many members until most of the posts disbanded. However, the Daughters of the American Revolution, formed in 1902 in Peru. Membership was restricted to women whose ancestors served in the Continental Army in the Revolutionary War.

The Benevolent and Protective Order of Elks organized in Peru 1897. Its members provided a great deal of flood relief during the 1913 flood and furnished window shades to Dukes Memorial Hospital. In 1902 the Knights of Columbus established a Peru council and in 1905 the Fraternal Order of Eagles organized in Peru. The Young Men's Christian Association formed in Peru around 1900 and the YMCA building was built shortly thereafter. When first established the association was intended as a railroad men's organization, but after a few years membership was extended to others.

The Peru Mothers Club organized in 1913 "for the study and discussion of problems of interest to mothers and housewives." In later years the Peru Grandmothers Club organized along with a number of homemaker extension clubs. In 1914 the Peru Country Club organized. Since then, a number of social and service organizations have sprung up in Miami County. Among them are the Miami County Genealogical Society, the Women's Literary Club, Ringmasters Chorus, Tri Kappa Sorority, Miami County Symphony Unit, American Legion posts, Hodgini-Wilno Tent No. 161 of Circus Fans of America, the Circus Parents Club, the Disabled American Veterans chapter, Altrusa, Lions Clubs, and others too numerous to mention.

Over sixty businesses were represented in this turn-of-the-century merchants' carnival. Courtesy of the Miami County Historical Society.

There are the festivals, large and small, modern and historical, that draw people. Some have been ongoing for years with roots stretching back to even earlier days and events. Others, like Bunker Hill's Squirrel Village Festival, have been started only recently. John and Janet Riggle, founders of the festival named for a Potawatomi Indian with a village near Bunker Hill, didn't realize how much Indian history Indiana or Miami County possessed until they began researching. "I guess you picture Indians out like in Wyoming, but not right here in Indiana. But a lot of famous battles between Indians and pioneers took place right here on Indiana soil," said Janet Riggle in 1993.

These were unidentified members of Waupecong's coronet band. Courtesy of Frank Whiterd.

Miami County has had a rich and diverse history whether one speaks of its leisure activities, women of distinction, or its founding fathers. But history often began, not with the laying out of towns or performance of unusual deeds, but with the forming of families and the building of their homes so they could stay and live in the new county. Sometimes the families were rich and famous and their homes a showcase. Sometimes the families were ordinary people just trying to make a good life in a humble abode. And sometimes one man's home became his castle.

The Mongosia Tribe No. 267 Improved Order of Red Man, formed at Miami, was named for John Mongosia, a Miami Indian. The Meshingomesia Tribe, No. 235, was founded in Peru in 1897, the same year the Miamis lost federal recognition as a tribe. Courtesy of the Miami County Historical Society.

The Peru Baptist Boys Brigade was at Camp Cooper near Chili in 1901 when they heard President William McKinley was almost assassinated. Courtesy of the Miami County Historical Society.

These members of Denver's Mandolin Society were photographed about 1906. Courtesy of the Miami County Historical Society.

Rambler Cycle Club members posed in front of their club house. Cycling was a favorite pastime in the early years of this century. Courtesy of the Miami County Historical Society.

Parades of any kind brought out the crowds. This was a Labor Day parade in Peru around 1900. Courtesy of the Miami County Historical Society.

This photograph, taken in 1909 for a doctors' and lawyers' charity baseball game, was titled "A Ton of Doctors." The dog had to be included to "make" the ton. Standing from left to right are: Doctors C. E. Goodrich, C. E. Redmon, L. O. Malsbury, P. B. Carter, J. E. Yarling, and Jared Spooner. Sitting from left to right are: Doctors J. B. Higgins, O. U. Carl, Tom Naughton, and W. R. Meeker. The dog may have belonged to Higgins. The doctors won the game. Courtesy of the Miami County Historical Society.

Some early Miami County Boy Scouts camped out under a large tent. Courtesy of the Miami County Historical Society.

These people skated on the Eel River, possibly near Mexico. Courtesy of the Miami County Historical Society.

The Victoria Theatre stood on south Broadway where the Elbow Bender Saloon is now. Courtesy of the Miami County Historical Society.

This photograph of the Deedsville band was taken about 1915. From left to right, back row, are: Asher Lockwood, Leander Leedy, Berchard Leedy, Will Waymire, Odie Hart, an unidentified man, Ross Robbins, Owen Cripe, Waldo Lockwood, Elgie Han, Alfey Evans, and Vere Bolden. Seated left to right are: Clarence Robins, Clarence Hattery, Claude Kindig, Murray Wildman, Willard Buck, Dewey Dawalt, an unidentified man, Elner Conner, and Russell Fritz. Courtesy of the Miami County Historical Society.

Members of the Moseley and Garver families went fishing in this undated photograph. Courtesy of the Louanna Wilson Estate.

Dozens upon dozens of people gathered for this picnic at Maconaquah Park. Picnics were a favorite pastime. Courtesy of the Miami County Historical Society.

Bryan Steam employees dressed up as women and entertained in this undated photograph. Courtesy of the Miami County Historical Society.

This child and young canine companion stopped their play with a wagon to pose with the chickens. Courtesy of the Miami County Historical Society.

CHAPTER 14

Homes and Families

Yvonne Hilgeman first thought she was uncovering someone's larger-than-life scribbles on a wall in her Peru home when she stripped off seven layers of wallpaper and two layers of paint. The scribbles, when fully revealed by her husband, turned out to be charcoal drawings of a dog, the head and shoulders of a man, the head, shoulders and torso of another man, and two signatures—George Eckstein and Fred Eckstein—and a date: January 24, 1893. "When we bought the house in 1988, its age was listed as 'unknown.' So it was kind of exciting to uncover a date and know when the house was standing," said Yvonne Hilgeman in 1994.

Miami County residents occasionally discover fascinating things about their homes. They may find their homes to be former one-room schoolhouses, large Victorian beauties with vintage toys from the 1930s forgotten in attic boxes, or places where circus stars stayed for a time. Homes today might have been past residences of former wealthy or famous families, of long ago Miami Indian chiefs, and possible hiding places for slaves escaping north on the Underground Railroad.

The first homes built in Miami County were virtually all log cabins because of an abundance of materials and the lack of sawmills to provide cut lumber. As the years passed, the Wabash and Erie Canal provided a way to export and import goods from the East. Prosperity allowed farmers, merchants, and others to build timber frame homes and later brick ones. The establishment of three major rail lines in Peru produced a boom in business and industries. The era of the "Victorians" had arrived, and they built many beautiful homes of that period. Greek Revival, Italianate, Second Empire, and Queen Anne are some of the other beautiful architectural styles that can still be seen throughout the county in homes and business buildings today. As one Ridgeview student, Helen Personett, wrote about the Zerns' old stone house:

This house, built by the U.S. government for Miami Chief John B. Richardville in 1828, was bought by John and Linda Gustin who restored it. The house stands just off Indiana 124 and back from County Road 300 East. Part of the property forms the site of Osage Village, one of the largest and most important Miami Indian villages. It was burned around 1812. Osage Rock marks the spot where Chief Tecumseh met with other tribes to declare war on the whites. The Indiana Historical Bureau donated a marker to honor Richardville. "Everything is a historical occasion, but this is especially one. An occasion like this ties us all together: those who have gone before, the present generations, and those as yet unborn," said Wap Shing, Miami spiritual leader.

What do you see when this home appears

Beside life's busy way?

Only a home grown gray with years

As men themselves grow gray?

I see the home of pioneers

Who gave us yesterday.

The former Mary Schmidt and Godlove Conradt posed for this photograph on their wedding day, December 27, 1857. Conradt, whose father established a Peru tannery, came to America from Germany at age six. Due to Godlove's business sense, the tannery reportedly became one of the largest in northern Indiana. Courtesy of the Miami County Historical Society.

Mary and Godlove Conradt lived in this brick home at the corner of Miami and Sixth Streets in Peru. The house still stands today. Courtesy of the Miami County Historical Society.

These two unidentified men enjoyed music together. Courtesy of the Miami County Historical Society.

The Northern Indiana Public Service Company probably set up this window display of a Peru kitchen, circa 1860s, during Peru's centennial in 1948. Note the water pump and tub on the left, a butter churn against the back wall, and the iron stove on the right. Courtesy of the Miami County Historical Society.

A PERU KITCHEN

The old Zern home stood on West Main Street. The two eldest Zern brothers, Henry and George, came from Pennsylvania to Peru in the early 1830s and established homes for themselves before their parents and siblings followed about 1836. Courtesy of the Miami County Historical Society.

George and Mary Zern, who traveled from Pennsylvania with the ten youngest of their twelve children, built the two-and-a-half-story stone house about three miles west of Peru along the Wabash and Erie Canal about 1836. In a time when single-story log cabins with ladders leading up to sleeping lofts usually comprised a home, the stone house with its staircase attracted visitors from miles around. Harriet, the youngest Zern daughter, entertained her children and grandchildren with tales of living out of a covered wagon while the house was built. Today the Miami County Historical Society owns it and has plans to restore it. Courtesy of the Miami County Historical Society.

This was a room in the Colonel Josiah Farrar home in Peru in the 1880s. Farrar was an attorney and Civil War veteran. Courtesy of the Miami County Historical Society.

Top photo: This four poster bed in the Joseph Shirk house at 116 East Second Street, circa 1890, came to Peru by canal boat. Shirk became president of the Peru Mercantile Company and Peru Trust Company, and vice president of Indiana Manufacturing Company. Courtesy of the Miami County Historical Society.

Some fifteen hundred area children were cared for at the Orphans' Home in Mexico between 1889 and 1943. Courtesy of the Miami County Historical Society.

The Salvation Army gathered toys and other items at Christmas in the old YMCA gymnasium to deliver to the Mexico Orphans Home. Courtesy of the Miami County Historical Society.

This was moving day for an unidentified family with everything loaded on the wagon from boxes to chairs. Courtesy of the Miami County Historical Society.

This photograph, taken circa 1909, shows from left to right: Lillian Clementine Godfroy, Swan Irene Godfroy, Gabriel Godfroy, and George Durand Godfroy. Gabriel's wife, Martha Jane Logan, made the clothes for the children to wear in Peru's 1909 Homecoming parade. Courtesy of the Miami County Historical Society.

Homes were ravaged and sometimes left tipped over by the 1913 flood. Courtesy of the Miami County Historical Society.

This family posed in front of its Perrysburg home, which still stands today. From left to right are Burton, Clarence, Susie, Lula, and Lucetta Green. Courtesy of the Miami County Historical Society.

This photograph of an unidentified Miller family farm in winter was taken about 1918. Courtesy of the Miami County Historical Society.

These women came together for a once common pastime—
a quilting bee. From left to right are: a woman by the last
name of Moseley, either Mary Moseley or Ella Mullikin,
Lydia Cook, Maggie Carson, Mary Rouch, and "Grandma"
Moseley. Courtesy of the Louanna Wilson Estate.

These two women and a child in stylish attire pose
on a downtown street. Courtesy of the Miami County
Historical Society.

These unidentified Bunker Hill women were probably making apple butter. Courtesy of the Miami County Historical Society.

These unidentified women were having wash day. Courtesy of the Miami County Historical Society.

These women were on their way out to empty chamber pots. Chamber pots were often used in bedrooms before indoor plumbing when people didn't want to go to the outhouse. Courtesy of the Miami County Historical Society.

This unidentified Bunker Hill man was photographed going into an outhouse. Outhouses remained in fairly common use through the 1930s. Courtesy of the Miami County Historical Society.

Tuk-Da-Wa Gardens was the home of Russell Jones and family two miles north of Peru along State Road 19 in the 1930s and 1940s. Jones grew thousands of peonies, poppies, and other flowers of which he sold bulbs in the spring. He studied flowers for years and worked in the hardware business with his brother, Clifford. Courtesy of the Miami County Historical Society.

This unidentified family pose in their automobile with the top down and a Miller's Garage of Converse ribbon hanging over the door. Courtesy of the Miami County Historical Society.

Mary Struble Reynolds married a wealthy physician in 1870 and later lived in a big house on West Main Street in Peru that became known as Reynolds Rest. In traveling around the world three times, she toured China, met England's Queen Victoria, and greeted Pope Leo XIII. She also visited Egypt where she floated down the Nile River on a raft. This photograph shows her on a camel with the Sphinx and an Egyptian pyramid behind her. Reynolds died in 1927 with an estate estimated to be worth around three hundred thousand dollars. Courtesy of the Miami County Historical Society.

Lorenzo V. Doud expanded his father's commercial orchard which was planted in 1894 north of Chili. The farm and the orchard, which celebrated its centennial in 1994, have remained in the Doud family since a Doud ancestor homesteaded the farm in 1843. Courtesy of the Miami County Historical Society.

Vyvyan Castle, located north of Denver, perches on a wooded hill above State Road 16. Wilbur Hunt and his wife, Jan, built the castle over seventeen years, styling it after William the Conqueror's English castles. Vyvyan is named for Wilbur's English ancestor, and family legend says that when the old lord lay dying, he decreed that the eldest of his three daughters—since he had no son—should make her son's middle name Vyvyan in order to preserve it. The name has been passed down through the family. "Every queen should have a castle," said Wilbur, speaking of his wife to the author. Courtesy of Jan and Wilbur Hunt.

BIBLIOGRAPHY

Books

Brant and Fuller. *History of Miami County, Indiana*. Chicago, Illinois, 1877.

Bodurtha, Arthur. *History of Miami County, Indiana Volumes 1 and 2*. New York: Lewis Publishing Company, 1914.

A Description of the City of Peru. 1897.

Ettinger, Mary N. *Mexico Home For Old Folks and Orphans Volumes 1–3*. 1989.

Five Rare Peru and Miami County, Indiana Books. Evansville, Indiana: Whipporwill Publications, 1988.

Gould, George E. *Indiana Covered Bridges Through the Years*. Indiana Covered Bridge Society, 1979.

Graham, John A. *A Pioneer History of Peru and Miami County*. 1877.

Hanou, John T. *A Round Indiana, Round Barns in the Hoosier State*. West Lafayette, Indiana: Purdue University Press, 1993.

Miami County, Indiana Schools 1830–1930. Compiled by the Miami County Genealogy Society, Kokomo, Indiana: Selby and Printing, 1984.

Public Schools of the City of Peru, Indiana 1899–1900. A Peru Public Library reproduction, 1985.

The Soldiers. Editors of Time-Life Books with text by David Nevin. Alexandria, Virginia: Time-Life Books, Inc., 1974.

Stephens. *History of Miami County*.

Weldon, DeLoris. *The First 25 Years*. Peru, Indiana: Modern Graphics, 1985.

Articles and Pamphlets

Andrews, C. Y. *Maconaquah*. Peru, Indiana: Sentinel Printing Company, 1927.

"A Town Called Cucumber," *The Elks Magazine*. Chicago, Illinois: February, 1994.

Bunker Hill Post Office, Program and History. Bunker Hill, Indiana, 1965.

"By Faith We Have Come Far," *Peru Daily Tribune Bicentennial Edition*, July 1976.

Coppernoll, Marilyn. *Playing With Lions and Other Circus Tales*. Peru, Indiana: Miami County Historical Society, 1994.

_____. *Tom Mix and the Circus*. Peru, Indiana: Miami County Historical Society, 1994.

"80 Years of Circus in Peru," *Bandwagon*. July–August, 1964.

Fishback, Debbie Rose. *Our Circus Heritage, History of the Circus in Peru, Indiana*. Miami County Museum Collection.

Finance Record Cash Book and Daily Balance of Allen Township, Indiana. Miami County Museum collection, 1910.

King, Josephine. *A History of Erie Township*. Miami County Museum collection.

Smith, Charlet. "Here Abouts," *The Shopper*. Peru, Indiana: December, 1994.

"The Great Wallace Clown Ticket Wagon," *Bandwagon*, January–February, 1983.

Newspapers

Peru Tribune
Peru Republican
Marion Chronicle

INDEX

Marilyn Coppernoll is a freelance writer with a passion for history. She is a graduate of Peru High School and of Indiana University at Kokomo, Indiana. Formerly a staff writer for the *Peru Tribune* and contributor to the *Kokomo Tribune*, some of her articles have appeared in Dog Fancy, Income Opportunities, and *Women's Circle*.

"I guess my love of history started when my mother gave me a copy of *Frances Slocum* when I was about nine years old," Coppernoll says. "I love talking to people who remember the past and will share it with me. And I would gladly spend the next several years digging

through museum archives and reading old newspapers just to find all the interesting things I never knew about Miami County's past before. There's so much more to our county than just circuses, Cole Porter, and Miami Indians. There's material here for novels and short stories."

Author Marilyn Coppernoll.